THE QUEEN AND THE TURF

Helen Cathcart

THE QUEEN AND THE TURF

Published by Sapere Books.

20 Windermere Drive, Leeds, England, LS17 7UZ,
United Kingdom

saperebooks.com

ISBN: 978-1-80055-493-1.

TABLE OF CONTENTS

1: UNDER STARTER'S ORDERS

History is measured in the small event as well as the large and all the pageantry of the old-phrased 'Sport of Kings' was backdrop to the pearly June morning when the Queen came riding through the Windsor glades to inspect the turf at Ascot. The house-party guests, waking to the novelty of their Gothic suites in the Castle, were scarcely astir. The first royal despatch-riders had not left London; there was as yet no black box for the Queen to unlock and open; the daily chore of signatures still lay ahead. The day was beautifully fresh. First in a carefree canter, then a judicious gallop, the Queen put her serene mare, Betsy, down the course, her two attendants falling slightly behind.

> We went a little after the queen, and overtook Miss Forester, a maid of honour, on her palfry taking the air; we made her go along with us. We saw a place they have made for a famous horse-race tomorrow, where the queen will come. We met the queen coming back, and Miss Forester stood, like us, with her hat off while the queen went by.

So Swift had written to Stella nearly two hundred and fifty years before. Now the enterprise of Queen Anne and the enthusiasms of Queen Elizabeth II seemed to meet under the glistening, empty stands, like stage directors rehearsing in an opulent and deserted theatre.

With the morning dew still sparkling, there were only two gardeners, groundsmen, cleaners, and early morning police, pretending not to notice as the Queen appraised the going with Sir John Bulteel, the Clerk of the Course. Subsequently, at that race-meeting, the intrepid Landau won the Rous Memorial Stakes on the same afternoon as Aureole's photo finish win from Constable, a remarkable double that brought Her Majesty £5,175 in stake money. Queen Anne, in contrast, had inaugurated her 'new heat on Ascot Common' for a plate of 100 guineas. But the golden guineas have vanished from coinage and the centuries have rolled since Queen Anne lay a-dying and messengers sped south to bring her news of her last racing win at York.

Today the intense enjoyment and recreation that the Queen of our own time finds in racing is surely known to her remotest subjects. Queen Elizabeth II is the first British monarch in history to have twice headed the list of winning owners and the only monarch to have done so on a peacetime basis. In modern times, with the possible exception of the late Aga Khan, no other member of a ruling house has won so many races. Trainers and jockeys know that Her Majesty's thorough-grounded knowledge of bloodstock and, what is more important, her attitude towards the Turf, is almost professional. The ebullient racegoer who excitedly mimics the frenzied last effort of a jockey at Goodwood is the same expertly informed racehorse owner who can discuss Robertson's theory of male dominance or the Vuiller system of dosages.

In preparing this book I discovered almost a division of opinion between the properly reticent officials of the Royal Household, some of whom wished me to regard the Queen's activities on the Turf as essentially private. Historians, I fancy, will find it less simple to separate the smiling and eager Queen of the overseas tours and State visits and Guildhall speeches from the happy Queen who honours the Derby with her presence, the girl who soberly dedicated her life to our service and the woman who so happily joins in the traditional festivals of the English people. One remembers the breathtaking beauty of the young Queen as she rode in the great Irish State Coach to her first Opening of Parliament, outwardly as radiantly happy as if she were riding to her wedding instead of facing another onerous duty. Shortly after returning to Buckingham Palace that day, she received a message from her racing manager, Captain Charles Moore. A little two-year-old filly had come triumphantly home in the royal colours at Birmingham. The race was the Queen Bess Stakes and the filly was appropriately named High Service.

Discipline and relaxation alike are ineradicably woven into the texture of the reign. It has been pointed out that the Queen is the only member of the Royal Family ever to have found it worth while to travel from Balmoral to Doncaster and back to see the St. Leger, a round trip of 836 miles. However, when this was undertaken three years in succession during the Queen's acknowledged holiday period and yet aroused criticism, it was noticed that the Queen did not attend Doncaster a fourth year, perhaps for her own personal reasons. One can be too susceptible to the unmerited gibe, revived from Georgian days, that the Queen had visited Cambridge on her way to Newmarket. The Queen is also the only monarch who has twice held a Privy Council meeting at Goodwood House, but one doubts whether this justifies the twentieth-century critic, writing in 'a spirit of fervent loyalty', who considered it unseemly that the Queen should 'spend a week at Goodwood races' and took exception to 'the London season, the racecourse, the grouse moor'.

We may hope, instead, to probe the impelling inward motives of the Queen's racing zeal with loyal sympathy. One may remember that Queen Victoria herself once watched the finish of the New Stakes with such excitement that she nearly put her head through the closed window of the Royal Box, banging her forehead so sharply, in her eagerness, that she broke the glass. Nor was this the effervescent, newly crowned Victoria at Ascot who 'repeatedly during the day conversed with great liveliness with those around her and surveyed the races through a double opera-glass; and, if we are not misinformed, occasionally entered into the spirit of the scene, and indulged in a few bets'. It was the staid and practised Queen of thirty-five, more than a dozen years a wife and mother.

Prince Albert, while planning the Great Exhibition, appeared in the *Racing Calendar* as owner of another young hopeful, a promising colt. Forty-two years later, a horse nominally bred by Queen Victoria at the Hampton Court Stud — Sainfoin — won the Derby of 1890.

Thus one might as well fault the Queen of England for being English as for her persuasive addiction to the most English of all sports. In the pattern of her ancestry is kinship with John Bowes, who won the Derby four times, thrice took the 2,000 Guineas, and once won the St. Leger. Her Majesty's grandfather, King George V, was similarly acknowledged a sound judge of a thoroughbred despite his disappointing racing luck. It was he, in fact, the constitutional monarch *sans pareil*, who established in 1924 the precedent for a Privy Council at Goodwood House. But it is the powerful hereditary influence of King Edward VII which many people profess to see in his great-granddaughter's racing flair, although Edward did not own a flat racer until he was in his mid-forties, and his final trainer, Richard Marsh, found the eight royal horses 'a dismal little party' when he first received them for Egerton House. In his best year King Edward won only thirteen races, compared with the Queen's thirty victories — and £62,212 winnings — in 1957. In his ten years' reign he netted only £41,711 compared with the Queen's stake winnings of over £150,000 in her first ten years as an owner. Inflation affects these figures less than one might expect for, until recently, money prizes had barely multiplied by three. The Derby Stakes of £6,450 for King Edward's Minoru compares, for instance, with the £20,036 Derby Stakes of 1958.

It is fascinating indeed to trace the Queen's racing story, the first decade or so of her racing ledger, from her first half-share in a chaser to her eager attempt to achieve her own Persimmon and break a deadlock with a Derby win. We shall meet again the immortal Aureole, a horse who might never have raced but for Her Majesty's acute perception. We shall recall the strange story of the gift-horse from the Aga Khan, a foal to be looked in the mouth indeed, and no doubt hear tell of Alexander and Carrozza, the second-string horse who yet provided the Queen with her first classic win. We shall affectionately remember Landau and his spurring love of jam tarts, the brilliant prelude of Ardent and the ignominy of Choir Boy. Atlas, High Veldt, Doutelle, Miner's Lamp... Winners of lustrous fame, they come thundering on in a cavalcade of high hopes and disappointments, superb triumphs, and bitter failures. There are other horses also, never directly owned by the Queen but nevertheless beloved by her, magnificent creatures in whom she has taken as warm an interest as if they were her own: King George VI's Big Game and the runaway Hypericum, Lady Zia Wernher's Meld, the Queen Mother's tragically unfortunate Devon Loch, and many others. They, too, will be the good companions of our pageant.

The racecourse of our own day is never more thrilling than when there is a royal runner, perhaps with Carr or Piggott up.

For every follower there is an enhanced and happy sense of occasion whenever the colours of 'purple, gold braid, scarlet sleeves, black velvet cap with gold fringe' appear. For losers who have backed other horses there is consolation whenever a 'Queen's horse' is first past the post; the cheering is always louder and a tumult of satisfaction runs over the stands. The cry, 'Hats off for the Queen!' is perhaps seldom heard; there are fewer hats; and it would be a rash racegoer indeed who would fling a hired topper high to the winds for a royal victory. The exuberant bookie who shouts, 'The Queen, God bless her!' merely echoes the perennial emotion of the crowds. But the sun is shining, the royal colours are out... They're under starter's orders now and happily once again all's right with the world.

2: SUN CHARIOT

I

The first public visit the Queen ever paid to a race-meeting was on Whit Monday, May 21st, 1945, when she was the nineteen-year-old Princess Elizabeth. It was a day of brilliant sunshine and the Ascot crowds were in rare holiday mood, buoyed by the supremely wonderful fact that the war in Europe had ended only a fortnight before. There were to be no more bombs, no more battles. There would soon be no more partings, no more austerity. The throng was jubilant, and suddenly a shock wave of enthusiasm swept the stands when it was seen that two khaki-clad figures had quietly entered the Royal Box. There was a moment of initial doubt and then cheers broke out as King George VI and his daughter and the Duchess of Kent came forward to the rail and it was realized that they had come to share in the rejoicing and hard-won relaxation of the people.

The King was in his khaki Field-Marshal's uniform, the Princess in uniform as an ATS subaltern, dress of formal propriety in those days of mingled peace and war. The King had some doubt of attending the races, without the excuse of a classic event or one of his own runners, while hostilities were still raging in the Far East. It was evident, from the preparation of the Royal Box a few minutes earlier, that it had been a last-minute decision. The Princess had no doubt been persuasive at the luncheon table. Racing began at noon, but there were still three or four events on the card and the royal party arrived just in time to see Gordon Richards win the Bray Stakes unchallenged on Neolight, that dashing filly who was so rarely to be beaten.

The Princess was delighted. She was to be seen, asking insistent questions, pointing and gesticulating excitedly. She had visited the course and toured the administrative buildings when they were, so to speak, unoccupied and off-duty, concerned only with the preliminaries of a meeting. But now the spectacle she had visualized only in imagination, or had seen only on the movies, burst into life and colour, with the shouting on the far side, the babble of comment, the pageantry of the jockeys and their mounts, the ever-changing flux of the crowds. Moving down to the paddock with her father, her pleasure was surely increased when she discovered they were seldom recognized. Racegoers were intent on the tote and khaki was an inconspicuous garb when so many khaki-clad figures were present. The next race, the Finchampstead Handicap, offered her a particularly good foretaste of all the sensations the Turf was to offer, for it was won by Historic — son of Solario — after being paced all the way, yard by yard over two miles, by an extremely consistent rival to win at last by a length. The colt had carried nine stone seven pounds over the extremely long course, and as soon as his heavy saddle was removed he exuberantly rolled on the grass, to the Princess's great amusement.

Between the races, eager to see everything, she was privileged to enter the weighing-in room and she climbed energetically to the roof of the stand to share the view which staff from the royal palaces were enjoying with their own privileged passes, gazing down at the greensward that ran like a river between the great banked patterns of people. Then came the Bisham Handicap, to be won by Sun Up, and finally the victory of the neatly named Kingstanding in the Binfield Stakes. The King was, however, anxious to avoid an ovation and insisted on leaving before the last race. The Princess was left with a sensation of precipitant excitement and went home to a late tea chatting eagerly of the day's events.

The following Saturday Her Royal Highness was at the Royal Windsor Horse Show with Princess Margaret, and her entry in the private driving class, an elegant cream-and-red phaeton drawn by one of the black Windsor ponies, drew a prolonged round of applause. Without favour, the Princess won the trophy for the best single turn-out and, later in the afternoon, a painting showing her success in the same class the previous year was presented to her by the Duke of Beaufort on behalf of the Show Committee. In her happiest mood, the Princess was full of the superlative horses she had been watching, but still eager to talk of her Ascot adventure.

It became obvious that nothing could keep her away from the Derby any longer. In that most enigmatic of races, the King's colt, Rising Light, was to be pitted against an intractable favourite, a certain Dante. In the light of events we know that Dante was to provide the north of England with its first Derby triumph in seventy years. The curtains of the future, however, remained inscrutably closed in that June sunshine and Rising Light had convincingly opened the season by easily winning the Column Stakes to the accompaniment, as a newspaper reported, of 'much cheering and raising of hats'. This had occurred on the day when the Americans crossed the Elbe, driving forward their spearhead to within seventy miles of Berlin, and the topical ring of Rising Light caught the interest now that the lights of Europe were flashing on.

Yet, above all, a more personal factor created the Princess's interest. In a very real sense she felt that Rising Light was almost her own horse, for she had patted him at the door of his foaling-box at Hampton Court and led him on one of his first walks through the arch of the great brick wall into the paddock. She had ingeniously helped to name him, by Hyperion out of Bread Card, and was convinced he was one of a group of newcomers from the Royal Paddocks destined to affect the course of racing history.

II

At this point perhaps our narrative should change course itself and return to the mid-war period when the King was leasing the bulk of his horses from the National Stud and the fifteen-year-old Princess paid a visit to Beckhampton with her parents to watch the brightest hopes in training. Or perhaps one should glance back to the farther days of infancy when the Archbishop of Canterbury found the Princess leading King George V by the beard, pretending that he was a horse as he shuffled along the floor on hands and knees.

The Queen's love of horses can be readily traced to her earliest years. She was barely five when her governess, Marion Crawford, caught that first memorable glimpse of a small figure in the night nursery, the cords of her dressing-gown tied to the bedstead in lieu of reins, busily driving a team of imaginary horses around the park. Before long 'Crawfie' herself was a horse, decked in a pair of red reins with jingling bells, playing earnest make-believe in response to childish entreaties, snuffling into a nosebag or pawing the ground.

Around the topmost landing of 145 Piccadilly stood some three dozen toy horses, the stabled accumulation of many a birthday and Christmas. Every evening each fondly named horse had to be fed and watered, its saddle comfortably removed. Every morning each was set in order. And there were rocking-horses to be eagerly mounted in the nursery at St.

Paul's Walden, toy horses and carts to be drawn along the grounds of Royal Lodge. This 'obsession for toy horses,' Miss Crawford reported of her pupil, 'lasted unbroken until real horses became important.' Then there were the horses still to be watched in the London streets at that time, huge draught horses drawing their brewer's dray towards Piccadilly, and tired ponies dragging costers' carts.

The sight of a pony with a docked tail would arouse royal indignation at the nursery windows. The hacks watched from another window, prancing along Rotten Row, became better known than their ever-changing riders. 'If I am ever Queen,' said Lilibet, strangely, 'I shall make a law that there must be no riding on Sundays. Horses should have a rest.'

Although his granddaughter was only nine when he died, King George V contributed his own decisive influence. He was accustomed to go round the stables at Sandringham and Wolferton after lunch on Sundays, giving each yearling and mare a word and a pat. And his 'sweet little Lilibet' sometimes accompanied him on these expeditions, to be gravely introduced to Scuttle (by Captain Cuttle) who had won the King his first and only classic race; to meet among the foals Felstone and Polonaise, Etiennette and Jubilee (who was subsequently to take the first royal victory of George VI's Coronation year) and to see Limelight, the impressive stallion, one-time winner of the Hardwicke Stakes.

Grown-ups would attempt to urge a moral and tell how, as a racehorse, Limelight liked to begin slowly and let his field lead him and then come at the end with a burst of speed to win his race. And there was the Sandringham statue of Persimmon as a reminder of events far beyond childhood's memory, eloquent to the little Princess that horses, too, were often great.

The old King gave the Princess her first pony, a Shetland named Peggy, when she was only four. She was lifted on to its back and by her fifth birthday was a sufficiently skilled rider to make at least a token appearance with the Pytchley. Her father wished to honour one of the hunt servants, Frank Freeman, who was retiring, by having his daughter 'entered by the finest huntsman of his time', and for a few yards Peggy obligingly joined in the chase, so far as being led by a groom permitted. Henry Owen, the Duke of York's groom, found himself lavished with hero worship as the Princess grew a little older, accustomed to his riding lessons and well able to obey his constant injunctions to 'Curl in underneath', or 'Keep on your guard'.

'Yes, of course, Owen,' she would be heard saying.

On their long rides, Owen would listen for hours to chatter of *Black Beauty* or *The Children of the New Forest* and other books, and burs and galls and girths. When Princess Margaret was old enough to begin riding, Peggy was relinquished to her, while Lilibet took over in succession Gem, Taffy, and Snowball, a lively near-white pony of eleven hands high. She never forgot to stuff her jacket pocket with carrots to give Snowball after the ride. Like her daughter, Princess Anne, when balancing on a horse, Lilibet was completely without fear. On one occasion, when pausing after a canter, she let go the reins while placing one hand on the pony's loins. He at once leapt forward, unseating his rider, and the Princess fell. Of course, he was quickly caught and the Princess immediately remounted, saying severely: 'Snowball, that was very, very naughty. But,' she added, 'it was mostly my fault.'

Meanwhile, Owen could do no wrong, and was for years quoted as a minor family oracle with 'Owen says this...' or 'Owen says that...' Until, at long last, when King George VI was being consulted on some future plan, he told his daughter, a trifle testily: 'Don't ask me. Ask Owen. Who am I to make suggestions?'

III

When the family moved to Buckingham Palace, the toy horses were arrayed in the corridor outside the children's rooms, where they stood sentinel until after Princess Elizabeth was married. (Two rocking-horses long remained on similar guard duty in the friendly entrance hall of Royal Lodge, Windsor.) At the Palace very little time elapsed before the two little girls, in their neat skirts and jerseys, presented themselves at the inner arch of the Royal Mews and enquired politely whether it would be convenient to talk to the horses. This became the first of many visits when the two sisters would tour the stables and coach houses, making their way along the row of stalls, asking the grooms eager questions of the habits and characteristics, faults and virtues, of every horse. The staff soon grew to expect them between lessons and lunchtime or just before tea, when lesson books were closed. Thus early were horses identified with recreation.

In those spacious pre-war days there were no fewer than eighty-five horses in the Palace stables, and it seemed remarkable that the children learned to distinguish them so rapidly as individuals. Though most of those favoured, superbly groomed horses have long since gone, the patriarchal Noah lived to help draw the Coronation coach in 1953 when twenty-two years of age, harnessed just ahead of another stable veteran, the nineteen-year-old Snow White. When originally acquired from a haulage company, the latter carriage horse was christened Ballater, but young Princess Elizabeth thought him the most beautiful horse she had ever seen. 'He's so beautiful and so pure,' she said, enraptured. 'Cannot we call him Snow White?' and an enamelled plate with the new name was duly fixed to the back of his stall.

In the Royal Mews the Princesses also resumed their riding lessons and regular tutelage soon began with Mr. Horace Smith, whose school at Holyport was one of the Windsor amenities. He found the elder sister already a fine rider, conscientious and thorough, and he came under a crossfire of innumerable questions on stable management, feeding, and the methods of training horses. The Princess evidently found it advisable to check the knowledge she had already picked up in the Mews. As she grew in proficiency, the riding master tried her on a wide range of mounts, including many more difficult horses which she could scarcely have found a pleasure to ride. His pupil never questioned his choice or expressed her own preferences. 'The Princess was painstaking,' he pronounced. 'An ideal pupil, she knew that it was all an essential part of her curriculum of instruction and she was more than anxious to learn.' At thirteen, the Princess had already discovered her possible future position as Heiress Apparent of importance some distant day, as she imagined, when Papa was old. To Smith she shyly confessed that if she were not who she was she would like to be 'a lady living in the country with lots of horses and dogs'.

But the horses were already everywhere, horses brushed to the last hair waiting for her to mount and ride, horses to study and watch, horses of every breed to pat and admire. At Windsor there were the sturdy black Fell ponies, originally quartered in the stables though capable of living rough in the open nearly all the year round. At Balmoral she found the deer ponies to befriend, the shaggy powerful garrons who were the burden-carrying companions of many a picnic into the heather-clad hills, ever ready to nudge the Princess for titbits and often almost knocking her over in their curiosity. At Sandringham there were still many old acquaintances, though Judith and others had been shifted with the Stud to Hampton Court, where the high holly hedges were considered to afford better wind-shelter to the mares and foals.

The Princess began to learn jumping on her pony Comet and found that her Uncle Harry and Aunt Alice of Gloucester already had an unsuspected knowledge of technique. Aunt Mary, the Princess Royal, spasmodically appeared from Goldsborough with news of the Harewood racehorses. The Princess was entering more and more into adult conversation, discovering that amid the many fascinating new topics her own prime absorbing interest recurred. There was news of one of Papa's horses called Cosmopolitan who had very properly defeated another horse called King of the Air. On the day that Mr. Chamberlain flew to Munich, Cosmopolitan ran in the Hopeful Stakes at Newmarket but was sadly reduced to second. So that, people said, the Stakes were not so hopeful after all. Many months later Cosmopolitan won the July Handicap and the Princess Royal, who watched the race, gave her niece a warm description of his gallant and rewarding effort.

The King and Queen went to Canada and the United States in 1939, missing both the Derby and Royal Ascot, so that the thirteen-year-old Princess heard little of these last pre-war events in racing. Crawfie made sure of a long spell of uninterrupted schoolroom routine. At Holyport Mr. Smith noticed that the Princess appeared, rain or shine, for her riding lessons, but was whisked away the minute his lesson was due to end. Pursuing an exacting timetable, the studies with the

Vice-Provost of Eton College had begun and the young Princess was deeply immersed in constitutional history.

On one occasion, however, when the Harewoods were staying at Egerton House, Newmarket, the Princess went to see her cousins and explored the stables and yards where her grandfather's and great-grandfather's horses had been trained. Persimmon, Diamond Jubilee, Minoru, Friar Marcus — the men still remembered the old names with affection.

Inside the archway leading to the main stable-yard the young Princess noticed at once the panel on which had been commemorated in letters of gold the races and stakes won by King Edward VII:

Year: 1893
Number of races won: 2
Amount: £372

Year: 1894
Number of races won: 5
Amount: £3,499

Year: 1895
Number of races won: 11
Amount: £8,281

Year: 1896
Number of races won: 12
Amount: £26,819

and so on for a tally of eighteen years, down to the impressive total of 106 races won for an amount of £134,687.

Was this the moment, amid the friendly stable smell of hay and soap and fodder, on familiar family ground, the moment above all others that first saw the stirring of Her Majesty's Turf ambitions? Did she recall that tablet under the dusky archway, one wonders, when she was grown to womanhood and owned one of the finest racing strings in the world?

IV

'Who is this Hitler?' said little Princess Margaret, 'spoiling everything.' The war crippled racing and, although the Princesses had their ponies at Windsor, events were too sobering for wider interests. Princess Elizabeth anxiously asked what would happen to the Royal Mews horses and heard with satisfaction that they had been evacuated to Hampton Court. Even here the bombs fell, and one day a carriage horse with two shrapnel wounds arrived at Windsor Castle, where he was to be in the care of the veterinary surgeon. Princess Elizabeth was most concerned. 'The poor thing,' she said, inspecting the animal with real distress. 'Can he lie down to sleep? Or does it hurt him too much? Is there anything I can do to help?'

She made a habit of visiting the patient every day to help cheer him up until the wounds were healed. On a spare shelf, at about this time, she also began organizing a troupe of tiny china foals and other horses, a delightful collection she possesses to this day. Meanwhile a conference was held at Buckingham Palace to plan the wartime programme of the royal estates. Wise counsels prevailed and the King decided to maintain a small string of racehorses in training. The future of the British bloodstock industry was at stake, and the very normality of racing, though drastically restricted and curtailed, was held to bolster morale in the Services and on the Home Front in those days of ration books and blitzkrieg.

The skeleton of events that was evolved was the minimum necessary to supply the classic tests essential to breeders. The King leased several promising yearlings from the National Stud, and presently horses were once again an occasional topic of royal tea-table or breakfast conversation. As a result, Princess Elizabeth was soon watching royal racing events with particular intentness. Time and again she would burst upon Crawfie or Bobo, her personal maid, smiling with the news, 'One of Papa's horses won again today.'

In 1941 the colt Big Game, by Bahram–Myrobella, achieved a sequence of five successes, including the Coventry Stakes and Champagne Stakes, and emerged unbeaten as a two-year-old. Sun Chariot, a filly by Hyperion–Clarence, made her debut by winning the Acorn Plate at Newbury, then she took the Queen Mary Stakes at Newmarket and two other races, and finished the season at top level without sinking to as much as a place. Remarkably, both horses were bracketed together at the head of the Free Handicap with nine stone seven.

The Princess was permitted to read the trainer's reports, and was fascinated to learn that Sun Chariot was regarded as a lady of temperament at the stable. Like many great thoroughbreds of character, the filly could, in fact, prove mulishly stubborn, wilfulness that was often especially in evidence in starting or when the going was right-hand.

These traits were sharply demonstrated at Salisbury during her first outing as a three-year-old. After jibbing at the unlucky right-handed exit from the paddock, Sun Chariot pirouetted at the starting tapes and then ran with such disdain that she finished third to Ujiji and Mehrali. Yet this was the only race she lost in her entire career. The day before the 1,000 Guineas found her in a mood of such dour obstinacy at work that she could scarcely be persuaded to canter. Nevertheless, the leftward exit from the Newmarket paddock suited her so serenely on the day of the race that she won by an easy four lengths.

The previous day her stable companion Big Game had also won the 2,000, the first classic win of the King's racing career, and so Sun Chariot gave His Majesty a second classic within twenty-four hours, the first occasion a reigning monarch had ever won both the Thousands in the same year. The news of this magnificent double triumph of course made Princess Elizabeth ardently anxious to see the two horses for herself. She had just turned sixteen, old enough to register at the Windsor Labour Exchange but not old enough, it was held, to be allowed to see the royal candidates in the Oaks or the Derby. Happily, the Princess could exert immense persuasiveness, and her father rarely resisted her cajolery without some concession. In the end, to her infinite delight, he agreed that the Princess could accompany him on an expedition to see the horses at work.

All royal movements in wartime were highly secret, but an early start was made from Windsor, and the King and Queen and the Princess motored into the promise of a fine spring day. The exhilaration of such an unaccustomed jaunt with her parents, coupled with the first glimpse of the strings of trotting thoroughbreds on the Wiltshire roads, could alone have made the excursion memorable. Punctually at eleven they arrived at Beckhampton where Fred Darling, cherubic and apple-cheeked, was waiting to welcome them to the house. The Princess at once noticed his cherished painting of Captain Cuttle, sire of that well-remembered Scuttle to whom her grandfather had introduced her in early childhood, as if linking the present with her affectionate, treasured memories of the past.

Coming events may well cast their shadows. The royal party drove out to the downs where the horses were waiting to take a circle around the visitors before showing their paces. But Sun Chariot was in her most grudging mood and seemed determined not to be shown. All Gordon Richards' attempts to get her to start were unavailing. Presently she even went down on her knees, trumpeting wildly. The Princess looked greatly concerned for both horse and rider, though the imperturbable Mr. Darling took Sun Chariot's untimely misbehaviour in his stride. They could not know, there in the sunshine on the downs, that in eleven years another fractious royal filly, rearing and rolling on Gordon Richards, would sadden the Queen and at last bring the great little jockey's riding career to an end.

V

Among the many motive powers of 1942, Princess Elizabeth's infectious enthusiasm may well have brought to an end the implicit ban that had prohibited all royal racegoing since the outbreak of war. The King had to weigh a thousand risks of obvious criticism against the potential weapons of morale. The police had made it known that there would be a strict check on motorists and their usage of petrol, and many racegoers travelling to Newmarket by train philosophically had to face the prospect of a three-mile walk to the course. In the event the King and Queen motored from London for the Oaks, which was being held the day before the Derby, and their arrival in time for the second race was loudly cheered. In Air Force blue, the King gazed over a crowd thick with men in uniform. Fortunately for Princess Elizabeth also, a Friday afternoon was free of the discipline of lessons and the Princess was able to listen to the broadcast. But the radio commentator could not tell listeners everything of Sun Chariot's waywardness, and the Princess did not learn the real story of the race until her parents came to Windsor.

Three starts were spoiled as Sun Chariot stubbornly tried to ring. When they were off at last, she veered so far to the left that at least four lengths were lost. Nearly a mile was covered before she caught up with the others and made up for at least some of the lost ground. When suddenly she seemed determined to take the lead, with nearly four furlongs to go, she began imperiously threading her way through. With three furlongs she had caught up with the leaders but was once again running wide. Gordon never showed his mastery better than when he decided not to check her. Sun Chariot overtook Afterthought and then won by a length. A crowd that had groaned with disappointment now went wild with triumph, and much of the King's joy in leading his winner in came from the infectious delight of those about him.

Sun Chariot might have become perhaps the only horse in history to take the Oaks before winning the Derby, for she was still entered for the Derby the following day. The prospect was, however, ignored, and all the fervour of the first day's racing was repeated, with the royal hopes — and, one may be sure, the Princess's — pinned on Big Game. The King was again present and had practically convinced himself of a win.

But if this was the first Derby in which Princess Elizabeth interested herself, it was also her first racing disappointment. Big Game's success seemed a certainty to most racegoers, though Mr. Darling privately doubted whether the long run to the start would suit the colt. Raymond Glendenning, the radio commentator, had been asked to feature up the horse, who was, of course, the firm favourite as well as of royal interest. After a gentle opening, Big Game was sixth… Big Game was fifth… Big Game was moving up … now neck-and-neck with

Hyperides and now Big Game in the lead ... two furlongs to go. Over the radio came the cheers and suddenly the cheers died. Big Game simply fell back.

He was finished. Watling Street came up and took the lead over Hyperides while Big Game finished sixth. He was always good for a mile but the extra demanded too much of his strength. He was simply spent. At Newmarket the King was so disappointed that he had to turn away to hide his feelings. And Princess Elizabeth, for her part, was left to ponder the qualities of Fairway, sire of Watling Street, who had won twelve races out of fifteen, and the stamina of Phalaris, the grandsire, with his win of sixteen races. The defeat of Big Game on this occasion may indeed have led the Princess to explore the challenging counterbalance of the sire lines and the innumerable rivalries of breeding that constantly fire her interest and enhance the continual fascination of the Turf.

When the Princess resumed lessons with Horace Smith in order to take side-saddle riding, he was astonished to find her already a mine of information on current form and breeding, not only on the royal horses but on practically all the other two- and three-year-olds of other leading owners. Once again the riding master found himself rained with questions. The Princess assimilated and dovetailed facts with remarkably sustained accuracy. Big Game retrieved his reputation by winning against Ujiji, an old rival of considerable staying power, in the Champion Stakes. But what fine idiosyncrasies made the line of Blandford and Bahram to Big Game better than Blandford–Umidwar–Ujiji? What special traits were implicit in Big Game's dam, Myrobella, by Tetratema out of Dolabella, a daughter of Gondolette?

All these problems were fuel for reverie. Meanwhile the St. Leger was coming along, with Sun Chariot to be pitted against

Watling Street and Hyperides, the two Derby leaders. Through the summer the trainer's reports showed that Sun Chariot's temperament was steadily improving. Although it was annoying to find Sun Chariot quoted as second favourite to Watling Street, the race itself at Newmarket compensated for this discouragement. Sun Chariot early drew away from Watling Street and held a comfortable lead through the last two furlongs to win with consummate ease.

Now the King had won four classics and a total of £10,536 in stakes, bringing him to the head of the winning owners of the year. There is a story that Princess Elizabeth had encouraged her father to take her to Beckhampton by promising him, 'I will bring you luck!' and certainly his success kindled her interest as disastrous failure might never have done. 'She is a fiend about horses,' it is recorded that the King told a friend at about this time. At all events, the Princess's early promptings made His Majesty decide to breed his own horses again and bring back into use the foaling-boxes that had been empty — or at least in semi-disuse — too long at Hampton Court.

The mare Bread Card — out of Popinjay, one of the three foundation mares of the famous Cliveden Stud — had been purchased for the Royal Paddocks from Lord Astor, and shortly before the St. Leger the Princess Elizabeth heard of her foaling by Hyperion. She paid a visit to Hampton that same week to watch the newcomer, Rising Light, staggering enchantingly in the deep straw of the foaling yard. The head groom, a Northamptonshire veteran who had served under Edward VII at Sandringham, respectfully agreed that a son of Hyperion, leading sire of the past three years, must indeed be *worth* watching. He could remember Hyperion's Derby-winning great-grandsire Minoru, and now with some pride the old man positioned the new foal to be photographed by King Edward VII's great-granddaughter.

This was the prelude to many visits Her Royal Highness paid to the thoroughbred stud. She always made a point of telephoning beforehand to enquire whether it would be convenient, it was noticed, and she never ventured to wander even in this tranquil royal domain without first politely presenting herself to Captain Charles Moore or his assistant. The Princess liked to spend an afternoon strolling from paddock to paddock — fifteen in all, spread over seventy-five acres — but she disliked taking up the time of the staff, who were overworked by war duties, and would insist on opening and closing the gates herself as she made her round of inspection. The mares soon learned to welcome her and would come galloping up, aware that her handbag contained an apparently endless supply of carrots. Sometimes Princess Margaret accompanied Princess Elizabeth on these expeditions, and it is fortunate that the sisters shared a passion for horses and photography, such was the time taken up in awaiting the right light and just the right stance. The foals at Hampton are led on a light rein when only three or four days old and by stages grow accustomed to a head collar within two or three weeks. Rising Light was charmingly photographed at every phase of development, forming a set of the Queen's early snapshots in what has become one of the finest private collections of racing photographs in Britain.

Touring the sheds, the Princess would also knowledgeably discuss the prospects of the brood mares, including Feola, who was in foal to Hyperion and was to produce a total of ten runners, eight of them winners, for the years ahead. Later on in the New Year Feola's filly foal was named Hypericum and with Rising Light and the yearling colt Kingstone, Feola's earlier offspring by King Salmon, there was completed a promising new trio to stimulate and deepen the Princess's interest.

Change was in the air. Although the King had softened the news to spare his daughter's feelings, tragic undercurrents had accompanied his racing triumphs with Sun Chariot and Big Game. Among his coming two-year-olds the King had focused some of his hopes on the filly Garter Stitch, and she was running well in the minor Wickhambrook Stakes, practically leading the field two furlongs from home, when disaster occurred. By one of the mischances of racing, her jockey changed his whip to the other hand and the horse instantly swerved, panicked and attempted to jump the rails. The next second she had staked herself and in her struggles injured herself so badly that she died almost at once. It was a completely unavoidable accident, but the discouraging effect on her owner was heightened the following month when another of the royal two-year-olds, Levity, broke a fetlock during gallops and had to be destroyed.

The King lost patience. He was not to know that Willy Jarvis was, in fact, mortally ill, and His Majesty was thus unhindered by personal considerations in electing to make a clean break. Captain Charles Moore was, of course, closely consulted in the choice of a new royal trainer and it seems unlikely that Princess Elizabeth did not join in the family breakfast-table discussions without expressing her own persuasive opinions.

The death of William Jarvis in January 1943 rounded off nearly a score of somewhat lean years, during which the royal horses selected for Newmarket training had been invariably in Jarvis' hands. But the King had decided as early as September 1942 to place his future Newmarket training with Captain Cecil Boyd-Rochfort at Freemason Lodge.

3: RISING LIGHT

I

Captain Cecil Boyd-Rochfort was already seasoned by twenty years with a trainer's licence when he gained the great honour of royal recognition. His clients included the Duke of Marlborough, Sir Humphrey de Trafford, Lady Zia Wernher, Marshall Field, J. H. Whitney, William Woodward, chairman of the New York Jockey Club, and Lord Portal, for whom he had won the 1941 St. Leger with the 10–1 Sun Castle. He came of a family distinguished for generations as soldiers and sportsmen. His father had been a major in the 15th Hussars; his mother evinced sport in her blood as sister of the famous Squire Cheape; his eldest brother had received the V.C. for juggling with an unexploded bomb, another brother had gained the D.S.O. and Military Cross, and Cecil had himself won the Croix de Guerre with the Guards.

He was one of the modern new type of trainer who emerged after the First World War, of impeccable antecedents, schooled at Eton, a younger brother who had taken up the Turf as a career with all the respectability that formerly adhered to the Cloth or the colonies. He was in his mid-thirties when he took over Freemason Lodge, where he quickly had some thirty horses in training, such was the confidence of owners in his skill. His first win was a Friday the 13th affair at Pontefract — on the 13th of April, 1923 — but it was luckily capped by a double the same afternoon. Earlier, he had studied under the immemorial Atty Persse and was a stable assistant during the regime of that phenomenal horse, The Tetrarch, who was the unbeaten winner of seven races and won £11,336 in stakes as a

32

two-year-old. Then he had the great good fortune as a young man of twenty-four to be appointed racing manager to Sir Ernest Cassel, and although the first war curtailed this promise it brought to Boyd-Rochfort strange links between Edward VII and the present Queen. Branching out on his own, he numbered among his first clients Marshall Field, whom he had known at Eton, and quickly found him a winner in a horse aptly named Golden Corn.

In 1937 Boyd-Rochfort headed the list of trainers and in 1938 he had cleared the remarkable total of £100,000 in stakes in eighty-seven races won in two years. Fred Darling was to hold the palm as the leading trainer of the early war years, but five of Boyd-Rochfort's horses won nine races in 1941 and six races were won with six horses in 1942, aggregates good for those meagre times. Besides, as King George VI studied the record of Freemason Lodge he was impressed by three wins of the Cesarewitch, two St. Legers, the scoop of the Gold Cup in successive years with Precipitation and Flares, the successes of Seminole, Brown Betty, Double Life and her descendants, and many others.

One of the first royal horses to arrive at the Lodge was a fussy, unreliable two-year-old named Open Warfare who by taking the Balsham Stakes at Newmarket in July had established Jarvis's last win for the King. But the animal dismally established little else and continued to live up to her name, by waging open warfare, as it seemed, on everyone from stable-boys to jockeys and starter. At Windsor she was one of the failures who gave both Princess Margaret and Princess Elizabeth opportunity to tease their father as the Bing Crosby of British racing. With Levity and Garter Stitch both gone, however, Open Warfare necessarily became one of the few remaining hopes of the King for 1943, and in April His

Majesty went down to Newmarket to watch this forlorn prospect at the gallops.

What he saw during the work was unpromising and Captain Boyd-Rochfort was unable to give encouragement. He wished to persist with the filly, nevertheless, convinced that there was something to be picked up. Persistence was indeed needed, and it was not until August that Open Warfare won the trivial Long Stanton Stakes at Newmarket. But this was Boyd-Rochfort's first royal success and with characteristic geniality and understanding of his trainer's problems the King sent a telegram: 'Delighted to hear of Open Warfare's victory. You must be pleased, too.'

The King had only three other winning horses that season, and the best win was Fair Glint's prize of £532 in the Littlebury Nursery Stakes. Altogether six races won by the King brought in only £2,224 in stakes. Yet His Majesty was harder hit the following year when Kingstone in the Gamlingay Maiden Stakes produced the only royal win of the season and stake money, incidentally, of only £262.

This solitary credit in his racing ledger somewhat alarmed the King, though fortunately he had to bear none of the losses that a more speculative-minded owner might have suffered. Unlike his father, who often bought fresh items for his stamp collection with the moderate profits derived from betting, George VI would never put more than five pounds on his horses and whenever he won he invariably sent the money to a charity. The cost of owning horses, however, was rising steeply at this time. With training costs, entrance fees, and forfeits, the customary 10 per cent of stakes to trainers and jockeys and the writing down of stud values, even the successful owner had to pay for his fun.

The Council of the Racehorse Owners' Association soon estimated that the loss on each racehorse could not be less than £500 per annum. His Majesty's horses, however, never cost him more than £8,000 in any one year. It was a not unreasonable total, and the King never complained.

The burly Boyd-Rochfort's counsel was one of patience. That it was a correct and prudent course was borne out by events. After the hazards of the 1944 slump, the King's winnings in 1945 rose to £7,736. In 1946 His Majesty won £16,528, a figure representing more than half the sum won at Freemason Lodge that year for all its patrons. There was a recession to £4,300 in 1947, a happy rise to £13,207 in 1948, a reasonable average of £6,788 in 1949. Altogether Captain Boyd-Rochfort won fifty-eight races for the King during nine years training.

But we have outrun our own course in assessing these soaring aggregates and should return perhaps to the calm day in May 1943 when the King and Queen quietly arrived by car at one of the Ascot austerity meetings in the hope of seeing the royal horse Tipstaff winning the Cranbourne Stakes. Unhappily Tipstaff reflected no credit on his owner and was badly defeated, but in the cheerfully fine weather Their Majesties contentedly watched another four races before they left. The story persists that Princess Elizabeth was also inconspicuously present on this occasion and it seems probable that, with her interests so caught up in the meshwork of racing, she was permitted to catch some glimpse of an austerity Ascot, probably grouped with members of the Household staff on the roof of the stand, where a good view could be enjoyed through binoculars though at a discreet remoteness from the public gaze. (It must be remembered that the German High Command believed the Princesses to be in Canada.)

Amid the wartime smokescreen of secrecy the King and the two Princesses paid a visit to Newmarket to see Fair Glint in a striding gallop against Fisherman's Yarn, Maiden Over with Kingstone, Crimson Lake with Esperance, but above all the Princess was eager to know how Rising Light was shaping.

This was the first time the Princess Elizabeth ever entered the stables she was soon to know so well. She spent a long time gazing at the decorative victory board near the harness-room on which are impressively recorded the names of the establishment's winning thoroughbreds, each on its own coloured disc framed in a horse's shoe. With Mrs. Boyd-Rochfort, she looked at the portraits of the stable's past stars, asking many eager questions on the abilities of horses that had raced during her early schooldays. The Princess made no secret of her Derby aspirations for the untried Rising Light. 'He is almost my very own horse,' she confided.

Two or three weeks before the Kingstone triumph that produced the solitary royal racing win of 1944, Rising Light made his debut at Newmarket in the Isleham Stakes for two-year-old beginners. It was known that the Princess wished to hear the result as soon as possible at Windsor and Douglas Smith did his best with his mount. But Rising Light was not quite up to the going and, alas, came only fourth behind Sun Honey, the winner.

II

The racing events of 1945, the year when racing could at last be held free from the menace of rockets and flying-bombs, bears a golden glow in the sunlight of retrospect. In the early spring the Princess Elizabeth was fully preoccupied with her duties in the ATS. She was eager to pass on merit through her course as a subaltern and become more concerned with Army trucks than with thoroughbreds, with driving tests rather than current form. In the time that she could spare for sheer recreation, the varied panorama of the Turf, sharp-lit by freshness and novelty, nevertheless unfolded for Second Subaltern Elizabeth Windsor with an increasing breadth of interest. Rising Light so deftly opened the season by winning the Column Stakes, to the Princess's great delight, and though he failed to go on to win the Newmarket Stakes, an event which found him back in fourth place, he at least outran Sun Honey, the Isleham winner, and could be considered a reasonable Derby risk.

But the invincible Derby favourite that year was Dante, the northern horse of Matt Peacock's, who had won all his six races as a two-year-old, emulating his unbeaten sire Nearco. Yet you never could tell. After winning the Rosebery Stakes, his first race exceeding the mile, by four lengths at 10–1 on, Dante lost the 2,000 Guineas. Against the fact that Nearco had been purchased for stud at Beech House at £60,000, then the world record price, arguments were rife that he could not produce a stayer.

With so many puzzling elements, nothing could have deterred the Princess from seeing the Derby, with all the unalloyed excitement of watching the prime classic for the first time in her life. Once again the race was held at Newmarket under wartime conditions, for Epsom was still a shambles. Troops were encamped at Tattenham Corner, the Downs were griddled with trenches, the grandstands used as a vast dump for building materials, the totes had been demolished by bombs, the enclosure railings removed for scrap, and the weighing-in room was merely a stock-lined quartermaster's store. But the war was still raging in the Far East and the King went to Newmarket in naval uniform, indicating with royal correctness that he remained on duty, while the Princess wore her ATS khaki in which she had been seen on the Whit Monday at Ascot three weeks before.

They were in time to see Tehran winning a no-betting curtain-raiser and then both Dante and Rising Light received a great ovation from the crowd. As the horses cantered down to the far-distant start, the Princess shrugged her shoulders as if to relax her tension. Then she watched with rapt expression from start to finish. The field was well bunched when they appeared from behind the plantation. Dante was on the outside and Rising Light prominent, striding on, in the centre. Then Chamossaire was seen, until down to the Dip Dante took the lead, challenged by Court Martial, Midas, Rising Light, and High Peak. In the sudden final climb, it was Dante, winning by two lengths from Midas, with Court Martial, Chamossaire, and Rising Light as fifth. After a very understandable gesture of dismay, the Princess and her mother began laughing ruefully at the royal defeat. Yet significantly the Princess also immediately chose to subject herself to royal discipline and, swallowing her disappointment, she walked down with her father to the unsaddling enclosure smilingly to congratulate the owner, Sir Eric Ohlson; the trainer, who shyly tried to disappear and had to be practically dragged to the fore, and perhaps above all, the jockey, little Willy Nevett, who had achieved his third Derby win in five years.

The royal party stayed to watch Boyd-Rochfort's trainee, Battle Hymn, running in the next race — unluckily to be vanquished — before the King decided to leave, and then by a happy decision they walked down the course to the royal cars, tremendously cheered from the packed stands all the way. The Princess smiled gaily at the crowds. She had seen her first

Derby. She had experienced racegoing disappointment. And yet she had obviously spent an extremely happy afternoon.

III

The continual progress of the unfledged Hypericum at her gallops and the future prospects of Rising Light continued to occupy the royal racing ledger. Dante, Chamossaire, and Rising Light were all three entered for the St. Leger and Rising Light picked up the £258 Spring Hall Stakes at Newmarket. Meanwhile, there was some revival of Royal Ascot, with the royal lawn open once more, the Gold Cup on accustomed display, and the Royal Hunt Cup and Wokingham Stakes back on the card for the first time in years. Once again, Princess Elizabeth was present with her parents: she was no longer to be left at home. Petrol rationing forbade as much as a car procession down the course. Flowers were few, yet the crowds, though drab, were vast, and again royal weather prevailed.

In the Hunt Cup the Princess may well have noted the exceptional training that made Boyd-Rochfort's Battle Hymn clear the starting gate so rapidly that he soon had an unimpeachable lead of six lengths and was never caught. Before the Gold Cup she was able to compare a Derby winner, an Oaks winner, and a St. Leger winner, all in the brave parade. It was, of course, Ocean Swell's year, the first Derby winner since Persimmon to be successful in the race, as though mischievous imps were stressing royal success for the Princess's pride. But the Princess was clearly interested in the Aga Khan's game St. Leger winner, Tehran, and commiserated with Captain Boyd-Rochfort on the defeat of his Woodward horse Hycilla.

I doubt whether anyone was surprised to see the Princess at Ascot again with the King at the special meeting on the first

August Saturday, when Rising Light was due to face a small field in the Burghfield Stakes. One doubts, too, whether the Princess had hitherto had such a powerful swift jab of excitement as this race provided. It was Stirling Castle's race all the way until Rising Light put on a magnificent last-second spurt and caught up with Stirling Castle within inches of the winning-post, a certain photo finish if cameras had been installed at that time. There was a tense hush all down the course before the judges made their decision known, and then the sudden roar of enthusiasm for a royal win might have been heard at Windsor. The Princess was so jubilant that she took her father's arm and jumped up and down. Moreover, it was the Queen Mother's birthday and the day's sole exception to five wins by Gordon Richards.

It was said that the King shared the £762 stake money with his daughter. At all events, it had been another wonderful racing day, replete with drama and excitement to fascinate far less susceptible a racegoer than the Princess. Probably wild horses, let alone superbly trained thoroughbreds, could not have kept her away from the further Ascot meeting on the Bank Holiday Monday. Again, the King and Queen had no sooner arrived — with Princess Margaret this time — than they saw His Majesty's Kingstone sweep to victory in the Sulhamstead Handicap, taking up the running the instant he entered the straight and finally winning by four lengths. Again the Princess was overjoyed and the cheers and applause followed the royal party all the way as they walked to the unsaddling enclosure and back.

Already the trend was looking most promising. The King could afford to forget the racing losses of 1944.

IV

The tempo of peace came in swiftly. Relaxed and rested the Royal Family were at Balmoral that August and September, where the Princess heard with delight that Kingstone had won yet again, taking the Mapledurham Handicap from Cadet, Rising Light's old rival. It was Kingstone's third win and the King's seventh success of the season. The trainer's reports gave some concern for Rising Light's prospects in the St. Leger, for the colt had developed a small saddle sore. Yet Dante, too, was missing from exercise, having developed a slight lameness. The whole issue was in intriguing jeopardy. The race was to be held over a mile and a half at York that year and the Princess was keenly anxious to be present. Unfortunately, Her Royal Highness suffered one of her few riding accidents that year. In attempting to take a jump, she was unseated and heavily thrown against a tree. Both her legs were bruised so severely that the doctors advised prolonged rest in bed.

Princess Margaret, still in the schoolroom, was going through an enforced reading of all the works of Walter Scott. Princess Elizabeth took advantage of her rest to study Becker's *Breed of the Racehorse* and *Watson's Heredity*, and her maid, Miss MacDonald, made sure that volumes of the *Breeders' Review* were always to hand. Gentle family raillery assuredly drew some comparison between Rising Light's ailments and the Princess's plight. Both the Princess and her horse-by-adoption made a quick recovery. It was Dante who was scratched from the St. Leger, never to race again. Rising Light went on to finish second by two lengths to the National Stud's Chamossaire, with Stirling Castle running to precise form and reduced to third.

To top the season, Rising Light won the Newmarket St. Leger against High Stakes and Paperweight. As a four-year-old, it might be mentioned here, he was third in the Paradise Stakes at Hurst Park in April, a placing that thoroughly disconcerted his jockey, for the King had just presented Douglas Smith with a gold-plated whip and the jockey desperately wanted to win for his patron. Few losers have ever looked more crestfallen in the unsaddling enclosure. Then, in May, Rising Light won the £462 Chippenham Stakes in a notable duel with Stirling Castle. As a result he was put into a similar coup against Voluntary for the £857 Burwell Stakes and won. Princess Elizabeth had the satisfaction of knowing that her ward had more than returned the cost of training. Then he ran gamely second in the Coronation Cup at Epsom, third in the Queen Alexandra Stakes at Ascot, when there was nothing but a short head between the leaders, and in October he cleanly won £2,313 in the Jockey Club Stakes, climaxing what was indeed an honourable career.

4: HYPERICUM

Hypericum, that affectionately fondled filly by Hyperion–Feola, was at last primed and ready. Her Newmarket debut in the Chesterford Stakes at the end of August 1945, giving her second place by two lengths, was sufficiently creditable and a full autumn programme was planned for her. So the Princess learned happily that at the Ascot Heath meeting Hypericum snatched the one o'clock race, the Swallowfield Stakes, and then Fair Glint, a half-brother to Hypericum by Maiden Fair, took the 2.30, the Littlewick Green Stakes, an attractive double for the King on the same day. In the Middle Park, Hypericum was beaten narrowly by Gordon Richards on Khaled, but this seemed so sure an exposition of riding skill that the Princess became most eager to see the filly in the Dewhurst. By happy circumstance, this ardent hope proved feasible. The King had found great amusement in taking the Princess deerstalking at Balmoral. She was, he realized, now fully able to fend for herself and, besides, her encouragement accounted almost as much as Boyd-Rochfort for the dozen race-wins he had so far enjoyed that year.

The Lord Chamberlain, the Earl of Clarendon, was the genial spirit who waved the magic wand. Lady Wolverton invited the Princess to her home conveniently near Newmarket, and the late October race-meeting was to be the *raison d'être*. The Princess made the most of this generous opportunity. Though accounts of her appearance on Newmarket heath at dawn may be discounted, the Princess was certainly in good time to watch the Boyd-Rochfort string. Attended by Lady Wolverton and her daughter, Lady Hyde, Her Royal Highness was in the best of spirits. She had a keen eye for the yearlings, eager to know what Captain Boyd-Rochfort had coming along. She was perhaps seeking to draw comparisons between the Captain's general list and a newly leased National Stud string her father was training at Beckhampton. Courteously Boyd-Rochfort answered questions that may well have been ingenuous, for the Princess was only nineteen. Her Royal Highness took coffee at Freemason Lodge. Then she went on to the bloodstock sales.

This, in turn, was a superb new experience. Thoroughbred values that had till then been merely figures in a book became rippling muscles and gleaming coats before her eyes. Tightly clutching her catalogue, the Princess stood in Park Paddocks with the crowd, hazarding now and then a guess on the final bid to her companions. Altogether twenty-four lots were auctioned and 6,459 guineas changed hands in half as many seconds, including 1,550 guineas for Four-in-Hand, a six-year-old mare by Bahram. It was a morning of exhilarating, informative fun, and after a brief lunch the Princess was on the course in good time for the first race and not least the appearance of Hypericum in the Dewhurst, almost the final and not least vital of the two-year-old events.

After Douglas Smith had won the preceding race on Rustic, a Nearco colt, the cheers started for Hypericum when she had still a furlong to go, cheers that hesitated when the royal filly was almost overtaken, only to win by a short head. The Princess smilingly caught the trainer's eye. Classic future wins for Hypericum seemed assured for 1946. The Princess then went to the unsaddling enclosure to see the horse led in, the King's thirteenth and final success of that exciting year. Later that afternoon she commiserated with Gordon Richards on not getting the mount he needed that day for his 3,000th win.

Travelling home, the Princess could look back on another colourful and absorbing escape from routine. Already for the young Heiress-Apparent the skill, the zest, the intangibles of racing were shaping as steeplechasing had shaped a generation earlier for the Duke of Windsor, 'the one pursuit which gave outlet to my competitive spirit', as he wrote. A day or two later the Princess heard that Fair Glint had fetched 6,000 guineas at the Newmarket sales for stud in India, and there were several other four-figure items to help please Papa. One perceives there had also been much to tell a certain Lieutenant Philip Mountbatten. The Princess could look back on what was, in a sense, her first racing season, buoyed by a sense of participation in an exacting and almost personal struggle. And now there were not only the Hampton newcomers but the King's National Stud yearlings, Sun Chariot's first foal by Blue Peter, namely, Blue Train; Calash, a sister to Sun Chariot, two of Big Game's progeny, and several others.

II

The King took an Easter outing in 1946 and accompanied his daughter to Hurst Park to see Hypericum make her first appearance of the year in that preserve of three-year-old fillies, the Katheryn Howard Stakes. Hypericum had come well through the winter and should have been in top form, but she was in dancing rather than running mood and in the event was trounced by Neolight, Gordon Richards up, who was herself in none too good form. This scarcely enhanced Hypericum's Guineas prospects, but the King agreed to go forward. This decision was to provide racegoers — and the Princess Elizabeth herself — with one of the most startling spectacles of modern times.

Princess Elizabeth now had her own rota of ladies-in-waiting, and for official occasions her own personal standard would fly from a Palace car. When she sailed in the cruiser *Superb*, with an escort of two destroyers, to launch the aircraft carrier *Eagle*, the streets of Belfast were decorated and beflagged for what might be termed her first individual State occasion. Her Royal Highness now undertook military reviews, attended conferences and made her round of visits and ceremonial inspections in her own right, with full-fledged adult status. It therefore aroused no untoward comment when, after launching an oil tanker at Sunderland, she promptly travelled to Newmarket overnight to see the 2,000 Guineas.

It was just five days after her twentieth birthday and the Princess was accompanied only by a lady and an equerry. Her parents had made no arrangements to attend the Newmarket May meeting and there was no hint of playing deputy. For the first time, grown up, liberated from the trammels of her teens, the Princess went racing on her own.

She saw the 2,000 won by Sir William Cooke's huge and home-bred Happy Knight, a dark horse who looked so dazed and sleepy in the parade that the Princess could have had no special cause to view him with interest. The obscure colt won at 28–1 four lengths ahead of the Aga Khan's Khaled, but Sir William had backed his horse at even longer odds. As the Princess congratulated him, he bowed and said, 'Ah, ma'am, I've been knocking at the door with the breeding of a classic winner for a long time,' and they exchanged happy conjectures on Derby prospects.

The Princess relaxed happily in the atmosphere of the breezy Suffolk town. She called at Gilbert's to order horse-cloths and watched the Boyd-Rochfort second string at work. She was on the course early for the 1,000, talking eagerly to Captain Cecil

Boyd-Rochfort and his nephew, Mr. Peter McCall, his assistant trainer.

As at Hurst Park, the evident threat was still J. A. Dewar's Neolight, the odds-on favourite, though Lord Roseberry's Iona was also in robust form. Hypericum was second favourite at 8–1. But the odds altered drastically a few minutes after the field of thirteen fillies paraded.

Some onlookers noticed that Hypericum was sweating as she cantered down to the gate. The runners were under starter's orders, lined up and walking quietly to the tapes when she began to prance and rear. Then the next instant she bolted.

Charging the starting-gate, the strands caught Doug Smith by the shoulder and unseated him. Under the tapes and down the course the horse cantered riderless while the crowds roared with excitement. Perhaps the sheer volume of noise deterred the runaway from passing the stands. Instead, she turned boldly left and made at a neat pace towards the car park and Newmarket town.

Captain Boyd-Rochfort put his glasses down, convinced that the race had ended for him before it began. Policemen and others who tried to head off the filly all failed. Meantime, Peter McCall dashed from the club stand and rounded up the one stable-lad with whom Hypericum was always amenable. Giving chase in a car, they headed off the filly just within the car park. Naturally, all this could not be seen from the stands. But the stable-lad mounted and brought her back to near the mile post, where Douglas Smith had just stepped unharmed out of an ambulance.

In those few minutes the other jockeys had dismounted and the odds on the royal fugitive fell to 100–6. Some large bets were taken at 20–1. It was twenty minutes before the uproar died down, the horses were straightened and, at last, off!

Neolight took the lead. Yet the long wait had taken the bite out of her and in the final furlong up the hill Hypericum amazingly overtook, the bit truly between her teeth. It was Hypericum — Hypericum by a length and a half, then Neolight and Iona, leaving the elated Princess Elizabeth to walk down to the winner's enclosure not only to congratulate Captain Boyd-Rochfort and Smith but also to question the jockey with intense excitement on what had happened. As Richards mourned, it was an instance of the horse that breaks loose suffering less ill-effects than those who fret. And once again it was a clear demonstration to the Princess that a day's racing had provided thrills and novelty beyond the scope of any other expedition available to her at that time.

These exhilarating sensations were repeated when the Princess paid her first visit to Epsom and saw a 50–1 outsider win the Derby. It was a makeshift Epsom staged in dismal weather, but it was Epsom renascent with wartime disuse decently camouflaged and commentators noted how eager and full of excitement Princess Elizabeth looked as the royal party drove from Tattenham Corner in three cars down the course.

Queen Mary was there, undaunted by her eighty years. The Princess Royal and the Earl of Athlone were also present with the King and Queen. The King was in mufti now; the Princess in pale blue. Stage by stage normality was returning. On pure form, too, there was a piquant situation for the Princess, for the field included no fewer than five colts by Hyperion. The favourite, Happy Knight, was not of their number. Nor was the second favourite, Lord Derby's Gulf Stream. In the first swift hundred seconds of the running, Happy Knight was nowhere. At the last furlong Gulf Stream seemed the certain winner. And then suddenly the unknown grey Airborne emerged, putting on a magnificent spurt of terrific speed to flash first past the post by a length.

Princess Elizabeth still kept her glasses trained as the leaders slackened. Number 13 on the card, Airborne, was the prototype of all forlorn hopes, but he had been bred by a Boyd-Rochfort, Captain Cecil's elder brother. And the Royal Box had scarcely recovered from this excitement than there was another sensation. The names, Airborne, Gulf Stream, and Fast and Fair had gone up on the board. But it transpired that the judges had made an error and Radiotherapy was finally announced third.

It was hoped that Hypericum would add the £6,000 of the Oaks to the solid £7,000 she had actually won with the Guineas, and the King and Queen and the Princess were at Epsom later in the week to await this result. At the mile post the filly was indeed still in second place, but then she slackened and dropped back to fourth place behind Steady Aim, Iona, and Nelia. The 1,000 of 1946 was to prove to be King George VI's last classic win, despite hopes that were constantly renewed in the next five years.

Financially, nevertheless, this was the best racing year of His Majesty's life and he was inclined to say, half in jest, half in earnest, that it was all due to his daughter. Besides Hypericum's achievements and the prizes taken by Rising Light and Kingstone as four-year-olds, the new two-year-olds built up the aggregate. Blue Train, for instance, was tried out in the Swinley Forest Stakes, though he seemed so backward that Fred Darling feared even this late October event was too soon. Gordon Richards had summed up, 'I'm not exaggerating, but I could beat him on my new tractor.' Yet Princess Elizabeth was keenly eager to give the slowcoach experience. On the course, the colt seemed to be scarcely trying for half the distance but in a magnificent finishing spurt he trounced all his rivals. Calash, Sun Chariot's sister, made a flighty debut at Salisbury and experienced the rare rebuke of a slap from Gordon Richards when, on leaving the paddock, she gave a nasty fly-jump. Heads were shaken with still greater certainty after the start as soon as it was seen that a swerve was costing her lengths, but under Gordon Richards' astonishing command she finally made up for this misbehaviour with a comfortable win of a length and a half against fourteen rivals. It was indeed more a win for Gordon than his horse for Calash never scored again.

Historians will one day weigh the popularity of the King's horses, both the successes and the failures, and the general approval of royal participation in racing, as factors in the interplay of the social forces that maintained the prestige of the monarchy in the post-war phase. When Royal Ascot was boldly revived in 1946 with all the pageantry which the previous year had merely foreshadowed, it was one of many colourful yet dramatic assertions of continuity and national recovery. The King wore naval uniform, for he was convinced the grey topper would never return, and the women wore dark blues or brown under the lowering skies. There was no cream with the strawberries, but champagne had arrived and the still prevailing austerity five-shilling meal included roast duck and salad.

As in the pre-war years the royal greys were transferred to Windsor for the State drive of three open carriages down the course. Princess Elizabeth rode in the second carriage with the Duchess of Kent and, once the meeting had opened with the apposite win of Sir John Jarvis's Royal Charger in the Queen Anne Stakes, it was again noticeable with what exuberant glee the Princess enjoyed every minute of the programme.

Between the races she slipped down to the paddock with the Earl of Euston to study the horses at close range. Captain

Boyd-Rochfort was gaily congratulated for taking the second race, the Gold Vase, with Look Ahead. Sir John Jarvis was complimented for scoring a double when he won the Ascot Stakes with Reynard Volant. Gordon Richards was similarly commended when he had won both the Coventry Stakes on Tudor Minstrel and the Queen Mary Stakes on Apparition. After the Royal Family's departure, however, he scored a treble with Khaled.

But this was one of innumerable occasions when the Princess, after a full afternoon's racing, was still not weary of horses, for she afterwards went to the Windsor stables to see the royal greys prepared for the night. One horse, it was apparent, had tired himself in the Ascot procession for he stood in his stall, yawning his head off. The sight of a yawning horse was too much for the Princess. Convulsed with mirth, she went in search of her sister. This was a prodigy everyone should see. The Princess Margaret and the King and Queen all came to the stables while the fatigued Mountbatten was still noisily yawning, and the Royal Family stood rocking with laughter with the grooms and the stable-lads.

The following day the Princess Elizabeth arrived on the course with the Princess Royal in good time to watch the first race, although the King did not appear until just before the Royal Hunt Cup halfway through the programme. The Princess's assiduity did not pass unnoticed, and next morning the columnists pondered how long it would be before Her Royal Highness raced in her own colours. The Press Room half anticipated the customary libation of royal champagne to commemorate Hypericum's victory in the Coronation Stakes, but it was not to be. Her old vanquisher, Neolight, took the honours. The Hunt Cup, incidentally, was won by a five-year-old, Friar's Fancy, who was achieving only his second win and the Princess would have noted that he came of the same line as the great Sun Chariot through his dam, Fascinator. Current problems of breeding were soon to preoccupy her more intently, provoked by the steady stream of victories that French horses were already achieving. On the remaining days of the meeting, the royal colours rested on Kingstone for the Gold Cup and Rising Light for the Queen Alexandra. But Marcel Boussac's unbeaten champion Caracalla II, the first of his big post-war winners, readily ousted Kingstone and, what was worse in this supreme test of staying power, two other French horses, Chanteur II and Basileus, took second and third places. The Princess lowered her glasses with a look of dismay. Kingstone was fifth. The next day M. Boussac's Marsyas won the Alexandra in which Rising Light ran a valiant third.

Fortunately, Airborne won the St. Leger, a race the Princess was prevented from seeing owing to a heavy cold, although she had arranged to spend all four days of the Doncaster meeting conveniently near at Harewood House. Lieutenant-Colonel Harold Boyd-Rochfort and Lord Derby maintained their prestige above M. Boussac in the breeders' list. Altogether the King's home-bred horses, the thoroughbreds for whom the Princess had hoped and planned from their foaling, won twelve races. With the National Stud runners, His Majesty's victories totalled sixteen.

III

Many, many more French successes were to challenge Princess Elizabeth's innermost national pride in her coming-of-age year, 1947, a year that was to prove of such happy import in her private affairs. The racing trend was struck when a French filly, Imprudence, won the 1,000 Guineas, and it was already apparent that a formidable French invasion was to be a feature of the season. The Royal Family was absent on the tour of South Africa in February, March, and April, escaping at the cost of an arduous programme the prolonged chill of a severe winter that practically closed the gallops at Newmarket for weeks on end. At the King's request regular bulletins of racing information were sent in the royal airmails to the Princess, a thoughtful touch to help ease in its small degree the strain of heart-searching separation from the handsome naval lieutenant she had come to love. In a letter in that bleak era of frost and fuel cuts she expressed concern for the wellbeing of the horses at Buckingham Palace and Windsor. She returned thin and drawn beneath the tan and within two days, as if to typify her happiness at being home, she was at Newmarket to see Blue Train running in the Newmarket Stakes.

The King's Beckhampton colt had already cleaned up the Sandown Trial Stakes but he looked sleepy as he walked around the Newmarket parade ring. The going, too, was hard, a point against his preference, yet he strode away to win almost in record time. It was a warm day and the Princess had matched her gaiety with a delectable summer hat, which nearly blew away at the crucial moment and all but obliterated her view of the winning-post.

Blue Train's propitious victory was less pleasantly qualified a few days later, however, when Mr. Darling found that due to the hard going the horse had developed sore shins. It was feared he would run in the Derby only if the going were soft. The son of a Derby winner and an Oaks winner had never yet won the supreme classic and Blue Train was not to break this line of fate. In Derby week itself the colt was scratched. It was a costly disappointment. Instead Their Majesties and Princess Elizabeth were at Epsom to see the Derby won by the handsome French bay, Pearl Diver. The victory was greeted by groans, for the colours closely resembled those of the favourite, Tudor Minstrel, ridden by Gordon Richards, and at the last moment spectators were mistakenly cheering: 'Gordon wins! Gordon wins!'

Gallantly, too, the French owner, Baron G. de Waldner, sought to soften the blow to British national pride as he told the Princess that Pearl Diver was in reality English by ancestry. The sire, Vatout, was grandson of the classic Chaucer via Prince Chimay. The dam, Pearl Cap, who had won the French 1,000 Guineas, French Oaks, and Prix de l'Arc de Triomphe, came of the Flying Dutchman strain — and thereby hung another tale. Pearl Diver's grand-dam, Pearl Maiden, was a filly by Phaleron out of Seashell, a mare owned by a Suffolk farmer. And Seashell with her unbroken filly and two colts had changed hands for only £200 in a deal in a Long Melford inn shortly after the First World War.

'We must find out what happened to the colts,' said Princess Elizabeth, smiling as she heard this story. But Baron de Waldner had to confess that one had been lame and neither had ever raced.

A new chapter was opening in the royal racing regimen, for Fred Darling was planning retirement. Douglas Smith had also left Freemason Lodge to go to Lord Derby as first jockey and Harry Carr was riding the King's homebred runners, although his mounts were often all too inadequate. Prior to the Derby the French winner of the 1,000 Guineas, Imprudence, had also cleaned up the Oaks, despite the King's great hopes of seeing a win for his homebred filly, Pierrette. Although she was to establish a win and two places later in the year, she finished fifth under the eyes of the King and Queen and Princess Elizabeth. Though she ran well, she simply could not cope with the pace set by Imprudence. Another Frenchman, took the Coronation Cup and forecasts that Ascot would turn out to be a French benefit proved partly true.

For the first time Princess Margaret was included with the house-party group in the 1947 Royal Ascot, and very pretty the two sisters looked, chatting together with great animation, visiting the paddock dressed in their yellow and white plastic macs. Earlier in the month Princess Elizabeth had taken Prince Philip to the Hampton Court paddocks, a setting in which he had given her some instruction in the art and technique of an amateur movie camera. Now she also watched the races as intently through her viewfinder as through her binoculars, laying the foundations of her unique library of racing films.

It is to be hoped that this preoccupation softened the brunt of a tragedy the first day when Good Afternoon, one of the leaders in the Ascot Stakes, collided with the rails so violently that he broke his neck, one of the worst racing mishaps the Princess had ever witnessed. The gallant sight of Reynard Volant winning the Ascot Stakes for the second year running did not reduce her great concern. In the dearth of royal horses, the Princess watched with special admiration a Beckhampton two-year-old called The Cobbler and congratulated Gordon Richards on winning the St. James's Palace on Tudor Minstrel.

Almost without exception, the French horses paraded in sheepskin nosebands that year, an innovation the Princess was also soon to adopt as an owner. Their practical utility in compelling a horse to keep his nose down was demonstrated when the 25–1 owner-trained Master Vote wore one in the Royal Hunt Cup and won against the much-fancied French challenger, Patchouly. In the next race, the Coronation Stakes, his similarly decked stable companion, Saucy Sue, won at 20–1 against an 11–10 French favourite, Djama III. The odds interested the Princess only in tabling the relative prestige of the runners, but these two wins slowed down the French landslide and consoled Her Royal Highness for the defeat of Calash in the royal colours in the Coronation Stakes. Despite his utmost efforts Gordon Richards could not do better than sixth place for the King's horse. Nevertheless before the meeting was over the Grand Prix de Paris winner, Souverain, captured the Gold Cup — a French win for the second year — with Chanteur II second, and then Monsieur l'Amiral, winner of the 1946 Cesarewitch, ran off with the Queen Alexandra Stakes as Marsyas had done the previous year.

From Royal Lodge to the humblest home, the resounding succession of French wins was discussed with almost as many explanations as there were Chantilly winners. Had stringent corn rationing set up a time lag of malnutrition? Were we breeding too much from non-stayers? Had we raced too little during the war years? Were the sand rides in the forest better than the gallops on heath and downs? Did we try our two-year-olds too early? Such were some of the arguments of the year. The Princess became aware as never before of the range and intricacy of the problems with which breeders and trainers were confronted. Perhaps already shaping for her, too, was a dream of a royal stable of the future, a royal racing string that would restore the waning prestige of the English thoroughbred, a series of triumphs that would once again trumpet the prestige of British bloodstock throughout the world.

5: ASTRAKHAN — ANGELOLA — MARSA

I

On the day when the Court Circular formally announced the betrothal of the Princess Elizabeth to Lieutenant Philip Mountbatten, R.N., it seems strangely characteristic that the Princess should have been sitting in the Royal Box at the White City, watching the competitors at the International Horse Show, while her future husband was checking the preliminaries of a sports day at the Royal Naval Petty Officers' School at Corsham. Less than a fortnight later they were at the races together when, with the King and Queen during a visit to Scotland, they went to a meeting at Hamilton Park. Three of the royal horses were running. The King's Canvas Back was second in one race and His Majesty's Furlough was third in another, but the third horse, Carmen, made a poor showing. But even before this the Princess had spent a spare afternoon at Ascot to see the King's National Stud colt Howdah, and to watch him defeated by a sturdier Boyd-Rochfort rival, Black Tarquin.

It was fitting that four Windsor greys should serve the young couple, whisking them away together in an Ascot State landau on the first stage of their honeymoon journey. On the morning before her wedding day the Princess stood at a window in Buckingham Palace watching the fond, familiar horses being rehearsed for her bridal drive in the Irish State Coach, so keenly observant of every small detail that she noticed at once when something was amiss. Two horses, Angela and Lilian,

57

deployed as outriders to the team on the drive to the Abbey but Angela was missing from the returning procession.

'What happened, Major Hopkins?' the Princess asked the Superintendent of the Royal Mews later that day, and heard sympathetically that Angela had gone slightly lame on the journey down and had been withdrawn from the return drive to spare her discomfort. 'That was good of you,' commented the Princess. 'I knew something had happened. There was Lilian, puffing herself out all the way home and trying to make herself look like *two*.'

While the young couple were still on their honeymoon, the wedding presents were put on view at St. James's Palace, to be viewed during the next two months by over a quarter of a million people. With the pieces of furniture and the silver, the jewellery and the linen, the sets of Worcester and the sparkling glass, there were sporting prints of Newmarket, riding crops and sticks, binoculars, and other gifts that reflected the bride's equine interests. The Worshipful Company of Saddlers presented her with a superbly finished saddle, girth, and stirrups. Special sentiment focused in a good-luck shoe from one of Queen Victoria's favourite ponies; there was a sumptuous suede saddle, and an array of sporting books included Mrs. Wilfrid Holden's *They're Away* and Lady Wentworth's *The Authentic Arabian Horse* and *Thoroughbred Racing Stock*. With admirable sympathy, a Reverend Canon gave the bride a copy of Lyle's *Royal Newmarket*.

But there was one gift that could not be set on display: a gift shrewdly chosen to give the Princess the optimum of pleasure and happiness, as it was hoped, an offering fit indeed for a Princess matched by the standards of the opulent East. Meeting Her Royal Highness shortly after her engagement, the late Aga Khan said: 'I've thought of an unusual wedding present for you, ma'am. I have my eye on a filly foal at Sheshoon and have great hopes she'll win you a lot of races.'

Of all her wedding gifts, two thousand and more, none was probably destined to give the Princess greater anticipation nor, as it turned out, a greater measure of dismay. Her first racehorse! The filly was by Turkhan out of Hastra, and the Princess studied her pedigree with exacting interest.

Turkhan was the son of Bahram, the only horse in more than forty years to have won the Triple Crown of 2,000 Guineas, Derby and St. Leger. Turkhan had himself won the 1940 wartime substitute St. Leger and but for the monotonous repetition of the phrase '1940 — no race' in the records he would clearly have achieved many other decorations to his career. In the previous flat-racing season of 1946, Turkhan's progeny had won thirty-seven races in England and Eire, a precise parallel with Nearco as a winning sire exclusively on the English Turf. The dam, Hastra, too, was a daughter of Hyperion, the winning sire for the astonishing sequence of 1940, 1941, 1942, 1945, and 1946 and was thus linked with Gainsborough, Chaucer, and Minoru.

All this made a promising show as Princess Elizabeth expectantly studied the photographs of her new charge. Naturally the seven-month-old foal could not be immediately removed from the Curragh but the Aga Khan signed the deed of gift and directed that regular progress reports should be sent to the Princess pending transfer.

II

Early in 1948 the yearling filly was registered under the name Astrakhan. The Princess and the Duke of Edinburgh settled into their first married home at Windlesham Moor and motored to Windsor Great Park each day to go riding, always

59

methodically raiding the kitchen for carrots and knobs of sugar beforehand. Talking of Astrakhan, the Princess must often have conjectured her hopes for the 1,000 Guineas in 1950, though her racing interests at this time were currently more concerned with Angelola.

This big handsome bay — who was later to become the dam of Aureole, one of the Queen's greatest horses — was a daughter of Feola (and sister of Hypericum) and the Princess had first seen her as a filly foal at Hampton three years before. With a decided will of her own, she had never borne silk as a two-year-old, a policy which may have justified the form-book's tag 'Seemed backward' when she made her April debut at Newmarket and managed to run only fifth in the Long Ditton Stakes.

By May, however, she had made sufficient headway to come second to Gordon Richards on Goblet in the Haverhill Stakes, emerging suddenly in a magnificent dash from the Dip. Ten days later she won the Oaks Trial at Lingfield, taking the lead from Tesoro and Tudor Lady with such a rocketing burst of speed in the last strides that the jockey could not suppress a broad grin of relief.

Between these two displays of Angelola, the Princess and her husband made their justly celebrated first visit to Paris. It was a State visit with the usual round of inspections and wreath-laying, but on the Sunday the young couple went to church in the morning and to the races at Longchamp in the afternoon, where they watched the racing from the Presidential Box for two hours. Such an outing on the Sabbath made a clergyman speak of 'a dark day in our history', but the parson was perhaps unaware that the Princess's programme had been drawn up for her by her hosts.

In actual fact, at that time, the Princess would have welcomed any opportunity to rest, and the Duke was taken ill with some stomach upset but stubbornly insisted that they could not disappoint the crowds. The races, indeed, went almost unnoticed while the vast throng awaited the first glimpse of the Princess. The shouts of '*Vive* Elizabeth!' could be heard, it is said, at the far edge of the Bois. Yet the Princess not unnaturally looked fatigued until she rallied after a cup of tea with Madame Auriol between the fourth and fifth races. The Duke, although he felt so ill, outwardly appeared cheerful and smiling. The British Embassy staff had tipped him a horse called Whim in the fourth race. The Duke instead backed the French favourite, Rigolo, in the main race, with a small bet on the tote, and won some 2,000 francs, an incident which, widely reported, endeared him to Parisians.

Altogether the royal couple were very much on duty; the Princess had very little opportunity to observe the Gallic oddities of the course and this absurdly criticized outing was hardly to be reckoned among her happiest racing days. Next month, at Epsom, she told Richard Carver, the British-born French trainer, of her regret at not having seen Chantilly, and an invitation to visit the Aga Khan's stables there had in fact been regretfully refused.

On Derby Day the newlyweds again received a special ovation as they drove up in the second royal car behind the King and Queen. For a few minutes the press was so great that the mounted police had to ride their horses into skilful action to clear the way. Then, before the big race, it proved almost a strategic mistake for the King to lead the royal party on the usual walk down the course to the paddock. The cheers were thunderous and, amid garish but affectionate cries of 'Good old Liz!', a hectic scramble ensued when sections of the crowd surged on to the course for a closer view.

It was, of course, the Aga Khan's year. He took the precaution of flying his Chantilly ace jockey, W. R. Johnstone, over from France and his French-trained My Love performed a cakewalk over the Maharajah of Baroda's hot favourite My Babu, who in seven previous races had been vanquished only once. Apart from My Love, the Aga Khan also owned the 22–1 Noor, which came in third, besides a half-share in Royal Drake, the runner-up. The buoyant owner thus earned treble royal congratulations. Yet Princess Elizabeth may well have felt some youthful diffidence lest he should enquire after the progress of Astrakhan still further. The topic had come up on Ladies' Day, two days earlier. The Oaks was notable that year for the rivalry of Angelola and the Aga Khan's Masaka, a daughter of Nearco. The day was one of gales, driving rain, and sunshine, and on the road near Ewell the royal party had in a sense a narrow escape when an elm tree blew down a few minutes before their cars were due to pass. As it was, the road was effectively blocked and, to avoid a long detour, a police inspector asked at a neighbouring farm whether it would be convenient for some cars to pass through the yard. Gazing from her door, as the limousines jolted by, an astonished farmer's wife caught a smiling close-up of the King, the Queen, Princess Elizabeth and Princess Margaret.

Talking with the Aga Khan in the paddock, the question of Astrakhan was neatly turned. The little chestnut had settled into Freemason Lodge and she was very well. With that conversational hurdle cleared, the Princess settled down to enjoy the excitement of an Oaks which saw Angelola and Masaka far superior to all the other fillies, though Angelola was placed second by six lengths behind Masaka, with Folie II third. Some consolation for this defeat, in enhancing Angelola's stock, was however derived between races from the news that Folie II had been immediately sold to Sir John Jarvis for about £10,000. As it happened, this was also to be the sum subsequently paid for the King's leased colt, Howdah. One trembles to think of the loss to Princess Elizabeth after she became Queen if Angelola had changed hands at this time, and had never entered the Hampton paddocks as a mare.

III

That season Angelola went on to try for the Nassau at Goodwood and was once again opposed by Goblet, Fred Darling's own horse, who had similarly been vetoed as backward when first raced. Angelola led the going for three furlongs, but Goblet eventually won by a clean five lengths. Yet in August Angelola won the Yorkshire Oaks after leading practically all the way, and at the Ascot September meeting she took an early lead and won the Princess Royal Stakes, thus amending her failure in the St. Leger in the presence of the King and Queen when she finished seventh, just behind My Love. Finally she took the Newmarket Oaks, leading handsomely from halfway. Thus, before retiring behind the holly hedges of Hampton, she had won four of her nine races and had been placed honourably in three.

The King was having a good year. Though His Majesty had no wins at Royal Ascot, the fates being churlishly unmoved by the charming picture of Princess Elizabeth and Princess Margaret riding together in the second carriage of the daily procession, the King's two-year-old Boyd-Rochfort filly, Avila, later won the Waterford Stakes on Ascot Heath. Once again Princess Elizabeth could glance back at the breeding and rearing of a thoroughbred with fuller personal experience than

63

most people imagined. She could remember the arrival of Avila's dam, St. Therese, at the royal paddocks when first acquired from the Duke of Portland in 1943. Moreover, Avila's sire was Hyperion, and it was said that the Princess predicted confidently some weeks beforehand that the filly was just right for the Waterford, with its £803 prize. Avila's win and two placings out of four starts commended her as a two-year-old and, as with Angelola, her success foreshadowed racing events for the future Queen, for as a mare at stud Avila ultimately presented Spanish Court, Almeria, Alesia, and the ill-fated Sierra Nevada to Her Majesty's racing string.

Then there were the King's leased colts at Beckhampton, where Noel Murless had efficiently taken over, including a trio of two-year-olds whom Gordon Richards considered looked the best since the advent of Big Game and Sun Chariot. Berrylands, a beautiful colt by Bois Roussel out of Snowberry, won his first race at Salisbury and then took the Duke of Edinburgh Stakes at Ascot. Gigantic, the much-discussed colt of Big Game and Sun Chariot, half-brother to Blue Train, made his debut at Bath with Gordon up and stylishly won the Fernley Plate. But later that afternoon Gordon also rode the third colt, Royal Blue, through a streaming rainstorm and achieved a royal double.

Royal Blue, by Blue Peter out of Myrobella, interested the Princess Elizabeth as a problem horse, for he had twice been tried out at five furlongs, indicating on both occasions that he needed more space to win. In the six furlong Bathampton Plate he seemed to be nearer the mark, snatching a neck victory in the last few strides. Incidentally, Gigantic went on to win the Imperial Produce at Kempton.

Altogether in 1948 the King won thirteen races with six horses and his prizes totalled £13,207. His Majesty might even have achieved the best year of all but for the strange default of the three-year-old Open Country, a filly nicely named by Fairway out of Open Warfare. Open Country and Astrakhan can be coupled as the royal 'cripples' of the Boyd-Rochfort string. Open Country would never consent to be ridden. No matter with what care she was approached she would prance and whinny and no one could stay on her back. Even the weight of a saddle seemed to cause discomfort and a veterinary surgeon found pronounced sensitivity along the line of the spine. She thus never ran in a race yet the disability was not to prevent her later producing High Veldt and others for the Queen.

Astrakhan was an invalid of different calibre. As the question of entries grew acute, Captain Boyd-Rochfort could no longer disregard the doubts he had already expressed. The filly's forelegs were weak and she slipped her stifle, that is to say, an uneven muscular pull had developed and a kneecap was liable to slip. Yet Princess Elizabeth had many scruples against taking Astrakhan out of training, out of consideration to the Aga Khan, and a final decision was deferred. Captain Boyd-Rochfort no doubt found it a situation necessitating his best powers of diplomacy. Should he depart from his policy of training only the best, or perhaps tactfully insist that Astrakhan was a gift-horse to be looked in the mouth? In any case, his young patron could not be spared disappointment.

To resolve the issue, Captain Boyd-Rochfort felt that he could take no course but frankness. He finally gave it as his view that Astrakhan could never be trained with any reasonable prospect of merit. 'I am afraid she will never see a racecourse,' he said, and it was a view in which the royal racing manager, Captain Charles Moore, concurred.

The Princess had to put her own judgment as an owner to the test. With youthful optimism she still had faith in her horse, and was prepared to go to some lengths to ensure that the Aga Khan's wedding present should not only be raced but raced with success.

In the first days of 1949 the Duke of Edinburgh drove his wife over from Sandringham in a shooting-brake to take the final decisions for Astrakhan at Freemason Lodge. On the Heath they watched the King's eight horses at work: Avila, already well primed for her three-year-old career, and the new two-year-olds, Northern Light, Gaywood, Somerset House, Knight Commander, Hunting Song, Harriet, and Above Board. With considerable prescience, the Princess singled out the latter for special admiration. And then there was Astrakhan, her poor little weakling.

IV

Behind the scenes, Captain Charles Moore pulled the strings in one of the deft coups of royal racing management. A young chartered physiotherapist, Mr. Charles L. Strong, who practised in Welbeck Street, was called into consultation and gravely examined Astrakhan at the royal paddocks at Hampton Court.

Mr. Strong specialized in treating people suffering from rheumatism or sprains with electrotherapy, but he had also successfully demonstrated that horses could benefit, too. Astrakhan was an apt and docile patient and the Duke of Norfolk kindly agreed to lodge her at his own stables at Arundel Castle for handling by Mr. W. A. Smyth, the Arundel trainer, who trained for Lord Rosebery and Lady Irwin, as well as the Duke and Duchess of Norfolk.

So it was all satisfactorily arranged and Mr. Smyth took charge, while Charles Strong visited his patient every few days.

Astrakhan submitted patiently to the electrodes attached to her kneecap and the stimulating, corrective gentle electric current supplied, as it happened, from Mr. Strong's car battery.

The Princess seldom found time to visit Arundel. The illness of the King brought an unexpected burden of delegated duties; the Princess and her husband undertook a heavy programme of provincial tours and, with the Princess's anxiety to spend as much time as possible with her infant son, Prince Charles, while he was still very much a baby, bloodstock was less to the fore in her interests. The three-year-old Avila lacked a royal audience when she won the Katheryn Howard Stakes at Hurst Park in April, though it was a race the Princess Elizabeth would very much have appreciated. With only two other runners, the French-bred Folle Sultane and Tapiola, Avila took the lead magnificently below the distance and won by three lengths. Though second favourite, she faltered in the 1,000 Guineas, proving fourth, and neither the King nor the Princess were at Epsom to watch her in the Oaks, where she ran fifth. With Royal Ascot, the Princess Elizabeth, the Duke of Edinburgh, and Princess Margaret drove down the course in the second carriage and Avila happily won the Coronation Stakes, bounding home three lengths from Solar Myth. This triumph particularly delighted the King, for it was the first time he had ever seen one of his own horses win an important race. Her laurels thus embellished, this was Avila's last race of the year, after she had won over £7,000 in stake money.

Meanwhile, the Princess had registered her own racing colours, a slight variant of the royal colours with scarlet, purple-hooped sleeves, and black cap, and she was ready for any small service Astrakhan might achieve for her. The stable reports were encouraging. Though the little filly might not prove a winner, there seemed a prospect of place honours to afford at least a little pleasurable satisfaction to the genial Aga Khan. But he had, of course, discovered Astrakhan's failings and generously wished the Princess to take an alternative choice from four other fillies of his own breeding. One was stationed at Chantilly and three in Eire. Nor would he hear of a refusal. Grateful indeed for a wedding gift so cordially repeated, the Princess selected the interesting first filly from the young mare Bellinzona by Stardust. Bellinzona, a daughter of Bois Roussel, had won all her three races at Newmarket as a two-year-old and Stardust, the Aga Khan's leading stallion, had littered the season with a score of winners. The brown filly foal, named Marsa, was scheduled to go to Captain Boyd-Rochfort in due course.

Princess Elizabeth's racing affairs briskened, in fact, in the early autumn. Keenly anxious to divert her daughter with a fresh interest in case Astrakhan should continue to disappoint, the Queen Mother had asked Peter Cazalet to look out for a good steeplechaser, and on July 21st he telephoned to ask consent to buy Monaveen, a brilliant jumper he had been offered only that day. This presented a curious clash of events, for Princess Elizabeth's acquisition of Marsa was announced that very same day and it became a moot question whether Her Royal Highness would achieve her first race win on the flat or under National Hunt rules.

Astrakhan was soon considered fit enough to enter the Sandwich Stakes at Ascot, on Friday, October 7th. Yet Monaveen was engaged at Fontwell Park on Monday, October 10th. The Sandwich Stakes had been selected with some care as a race reserved for two-year-olds who had not hitherto won, though bred from stallion winners of at least one-and-a-half miles. The Princess had planned to fly down from Balmoral, and a Viking of the King's Flight stood by at Dyce airport. Unluckily, fog caused the trip to be cancelled.

In some suspense the Princess stood by the telephone. Captain Moore had shaken his head at so much blister treatment. A field of eleven presented sturdy opposition, including Gordon Richards on the formidable Watling Street colt, Golden Road. Astrakhan was ridden by the Australian jockey, Tommy Burn. But the line was soon open from Balmoral to give the Princess one of her most vivid racing thrills. Astrakhan was always with the first three and — it was a win for Golden Road and a photo finish between Astrakhan and Capricious for second place… It was Astrakhan second by a nose to Capricious, and the event ensured the Princess £81 12s. in prize money.

Nor was this joyful demonstration a fluke. Astrakhan was a 6–5 favourite at Windsor in the Upper Sixpenny Plate the following spring, against a field of eighteen. This time her rivals were Letter Box, with Doug Smith up, and Gordon Richards on Good Record. She was outpaced and she never challenged these two but she justified herself sufficiently to run in third.

The Princess was then in Malta, where she had joined her husband after the spring cruise of the *Chequers* with the Mediterranean Fleet. She heard the news by telephone and then fuller descriptions and photographs were sent by courier. At the Villa Guardamangia she was leading very much the life of a naval officer's wife, occasionally attending the small local race-meeting, watching her husband play polo with the Shrimps, swimming and motoring. One afternoon her husband was thrown on the polo field and she jumped up in alarm but he quickly called out, 'Nothing much, just a graze!' and remounted with torn shirt and bleeding elbow.

The Princess instructed Captain Moore that Astrakhan should be given a real chance against the best fillies of her class in the Merry Maidens Stakes at Hurst Park. This time there was no doubt whatever of her mettle. Burn rode her home superbly first in a field of thirteen, Astrakhan leading from three furlongs out and maintaining her lead with terrific toughness inside on the last stretch against Gordon Richards on Quarterdeck and Douglas Smith on Jessamine. The stakes win on this occasion amounted to £707, taking Astrakhan to the credit side of the ledger.

The Princess was jubilant. Was there even a prospect of Astrakhan in the Oaks? Captain Moore, however, took into consideration the quality of Asmena, Camaree, Above Board, and other runners and advised caution. Her Royal Highness accepted his counsel and Astrakhan was judiciously entered in the Oaks Trial Stakes.

There were only three other runners, namely, Harry Carr on His Majesty's Above Board, Gordon Richards on Sirocco, and Britt on Stella Polaris, the filly which subsequently came third in the Oaks itself. Clearly one of these entrants had to be defeated, and in the event the Princess was no doubt grateful that her father's horse came in second behind Stella Polaris. Astrakhan weakened to Sirocco at halfway and never recovered the lost ground.

With her filly's final defeat on the course, the Princess took the gentle hint. The Aga Khan's gift horse had won her laurels and had been truly proved. She was clearly not strong enough to remain in continuous training, but the prestige of a win and two placings in four races proudly enhanced her retirement to stud. In the lush paddocks of Hampton Court Astrakhan was presently to graze with her grey colt foal, Kolah, her filly foal, Kerry Hill, and others.

Curiously enough, the career of Marsa, the Aga Khan's substitute wedding gift, was far less distinguished. The little brown filly wintered at Freemason Lodge and made an early two-year-old debut at the end of June 1950 with Breasley riding her to the best possible advantage, but she tailed off quickly and was an also ran in a race won by No Appeal with Game Law second. Three weeks later Carr rode her in the Fillies' Plate. Sad to say, she seemed to be the last horse in and she died the following year.

6: MONAVEEN — MANICOU

I

It was early in the spring of 1949, when a disappointing future seemed in store for Astrakhan, that the Queen Mother first asked Mr. Peter Cazalet to look about for a steeplechaser of quality which she proposed to own in partnership with her daughter. Mr. Cazalet was already a model example of the amateur rider turned professional trainer: he seemed to have begun his career on the playing fields of Eton and to have diverted his energies profusely in cricket, squash, rackets and tennis until point-to-point and the hazards of steeplechasing claimed him to the exclusion of everything else. After riding some sixty winners in seven seasons he took out a licence and began to train for a few of his friends. The string grew larger and the momentum of his National Hunt successes after the war was impressive. Mr. Cazalet paid frequent visits to Ireland, and made two trips that spring without finding a suitable jumper for his royal client. Then, four months after the Grand National, he heard that Monaveen was being offered — reputedly at £1,000 — by a trainer of track greyhounds, Mr. Hawkesley, who had already won with him at Folkestone.

Mr. Cazalet acted swiftly, as I have said, so quickly indeed that the handsome gelding entered his home stables at Fairlawne within twenty-four hours. Mr. Cazalet had the tabs on his purchase. He could recite the chases he had won; he knew the horse held unofficial course records both at Folkestone — three miles in six minutes three seconds — and at Kempton. He probably knew that Monaveen had once been bought for £350 from a Limerick farmer, for the gelding, by

Landscape Hill — Great Double, was half-brother to his own stable kingpin, Cromwell. But above all he remembered every detail of that year's National, led by a horse which fell at the first fence but completed the course alone and won by a 66–1 agricultural show horse named Russian Hero. Mr. Cazalet's own trainee, Cromwell, had finished fourth. Russian Hero had fallen in his last three races and his dam had been bought for £25. It was the luck of the game. And Mr. Cazalet remembered with precision that Monaveen led the field after the first round and was still foremost at the nineteenth fence on the second circuit when a slight mistake brought him down.

To be sure, Monaveen had his shady side. He, too, had once changed hands as a farmer's hack and his farmer-owner had found him so high-spirited that he had harnessed him to a milkcart to tone him down. Plough horses and cart-horses have indeed won the National, and it is noticeable that more nine-year-old horses have won in recent years than entrants of any other age. Attempting his first Grand National at eight years, it could be argued that Monaveen, compact, alert-eyed, with the strong quarters of a natural jumper, had not come to his prime.

He stood at 16.1 hands, somewhat taller, in the modern style, than the stocky Ambush II which won the National for King Edward VII when Prince of Wales. It could be argued that history was due to repeat itself after nearly fifty years. Ambush II had once been offered for auction at a reserve of £50, only to be withdrawn and sold privately for £40. The price was £500 when Edward bought him. He first appeared in the National in 1899 and tried again at six years old, the second favourite, in 1900. His victory by four lengths against such Aintree giants as Manifesto and Hidden Mystery was one of immense popularity. Three years afterwards he tried again, carrying twelve stone seven pounds, and even so was being wildly cheered as the winner when he fell at the last fence, a racing disaster paralleled only by the Queen Mother's Devon Loch fifty-three years later. Sturdily observing the royal code, the King betrayed no outward chagrin but merely enquired after the safety of the rider.

Steeplechasing has a respectable lineage of royal tradition. As Prince of Wales, Edward VII acquired the first racehorse he had ever owned for a steeplechase meeting of the 10th Hussars. Edward was then in his thirtieth year; he had become a member of the Jockey Club seven years earlier, and the forgotten date and place of the meeting — March 31st, 1871, at the vanished Down Barn Farm, Southall — is of interest only as the inception of royal racing ownership. The Prince's ancient bay gelding came in second, and he entered nothing more until Alep, a pure-bred Arab of his, was beaten in 1877.

The Prince had to wait until nearly his fortieth year before he enjoyed a National Hunt success with Leonidas in the Aldershot Military Hunt Cup. It was another two years before his Fairplay won the Household Brigade Cup at Sandown. Queen Victoria's famous letter to 'dearest Bertie': 'Your example can do much for good and can do a great deal for evil... I hear every true and attached friend of ours expressing such anxiety that you should gather round you the really good, steady, and distinguished people...' This was an earnest and serious injunction that he should avoid attendance at Ascot on the socially wrong days. Edward did not venture into flat-racing until, spurred by Fairplay's good fortune, he acquired a half-share in the Oaks winner Geheimnis with Lord Alington. He put no fillies of his own into training until 1887, when he was forty-six years old. Meanwhile he began to try steadily for the high stakes at Aintree.

Queen Victoria, who was to indicate later that she might be prepared to watch Persimmon on the racecourse provided Persimmon would win… Queen Victoria must have read with distaste of the defeat of The Scot in her son's colours in 1884. For the royal horse to be favourite was no doubt correct; for the entire field to be blanketed in fog may have seemed to the Queen like the mercy of Providence, but to hear that The Scot fell at Becher's Brook and was defeated by a horse named, of all unutterable cognomens, Voluptuary — this must have wrung the royal mother's heart. The Prince of Wales tried again in 1888 with Magic, who stumbled at precisely the same spot as The Scot, and in the following year with two runners, Magic and Hettie. Hettie was vanquished yet again in 1890 and Ambush II's triumph a decade later renewed royal hopes in steeplechasing. On Ambush II's death Lord Marcus Beresford bought in the National winner of 1904, Moifaa, for the King, a seventeen-hand giant that Beresford described as 'the ugliest, lightest devil you ever saw'. In return for these ill words, Moifaa lurched and fell early in the second circuit. In the Grand National of 1908 the King entered Flaxman, a horse of acknowledged fine looks, but he lost the race when his jockey lost a stirrup.

These details have the challenge of comparison, as well as historic interest. King George V owned few steeplechasers, but a new Prince of Wales, later the Duke of Windsor, found happiness in the fields of Leicestershire, riding a winner over the sticks in his first race in 1921 when he was twenty-six years old, taking tumbles as an amateur rider that involved a broken collarbone, twisted ankle, and lesser sprains, and winning by ten lengths on one occasion on his own horse, Little Favourite. It was a steeplechaser of George V's, incidentally, named Marconi, who also bore the royal colours in George VI's first racing venture as King in the New Windsor Handicap Chase of December 1936. Unluckily, Marconi had no sense of his historic responsibility, for he lost.

And now it was another proud steeplechaser who gazed from his box with intelligent eyes, crunching the house-warming carrots proffered to him by a royal lady. The Queen Mother and Princess Elizabeth made a special journey to see Monaveen before the Court retired to Balmoral in August. The Princess was delighted with the prospect of sharing the joys of ownership, but practical difficulties soon arose and it was decided that the horse should run in the Princess's name.

II

Mr. Cazalet schooled Monaveen intensively through the peak months of the summer. The gelding had a superlative jumping flair but he had faults in technique and, above all, a refusal to increase his speed if he could see no further fences ahead. Many jumpers are apt to shorten their action after taking a fence, but not Monaveen: he could continue at tough, staying velocity and would lengthen his stride on seeing jumps ahead. The Queen Mother had instructed Mr. Cazalet, 'I want him to win, if possible, first time out,' and the trainer selected the three-and-a-quarter-mile Chichester Chase at Fontwell Park with intent diplomacy.

On September 29th, during a trip to London for the Harewood wedding, the Queen approved the announcement: 'Her Majesty the Queen and H.R.H. Princess Elizabeth have registered a partnership under National Hunt Rules of half-shares in the steeplechaser Monaveen. Engagements of Monaveen under National Hunt Rules have been transferred to Princess Elizabeth.'

With this formula Monaveen was entered in the Princess's name and Her Royal Highness hurried down from Balmoral ahead of her mother to see the race run. On October 7th Astrakhan had appeared as the first horse in the Princess's colours and had lost. To Monaveen on Monday, October 10th, went high honour as the first horse in the Princess's colours to win.

It was a day of warm sunshine under the chestnut trees. Little Fontwell, close to Goodwood, is renowned as a hilly and perhaps trappy course and Mr. Cazalet had put Tony Grantham on Monaveen convinced he could ride out the moderate field. There were indeed only two other runners, Random Knight, ridden by Jarvis, and Martin M, ridden by Major Blacker. 'Anyway, we are bound to get a place,' the royal owner joked with her jockey beforehand. It was not only her first occasion to see her own horse run but also her first visit to a steeplechase. Besides Mr. Cazalet and the Duchess of Norfolk, the late Lord Mildmay of Flete, that ace amateur winner of more than a hundred chases, acted as mentor. He had indeed largely fostered the new royal interest with his steeplechase stories at a Windsor house-party and now he effectively explained the diversity of the jumps, the skills they evoked. Monaveen's race opened the programme and the Princess watched every point intently through her binoculars. The bookmakers had little but her horse at odds of 100–30 in their books and the crowd groaned when, the second time round, Monaveen hit the fence before the stand right in front of his owner. But he jumped the remaining fences like the champion he was. Meanwhile Major Blacker fell and sturdily remounted and Random Knight remained in steadfast opposition. Yet still Monaveen romped home a winner by fifteen lengths.

The delighted Princess acknowledged the approbation of the crowd with hand-waves. 'Well done!' she gaily greeted Tony Grantham. Lord Mildmay, when asked by a reporter why he had not taken the mount, cheerfully explained, 'I should have been all too nervous.' Later that afternoon the Princess thoroughly discussed the future openings with Mr. Cazalet and, although she recognized the risks, she decided to try for the £2,500 or so of the Grand Sefton Handicap Chase, a drastic increase on little Fontwell's £204. Then, contented, she went to tea at Arundel Castle, inevitably touring the stables afterwards to see Astrakhan and to meet Crisis, a daughter of Hyperion; Zodiac, a Stardust son; Garrick, and other stable stars.

The following month the Princess was, of course, determined to see Monaveen run in the Sefton and she flew to Liverpool with Princess Margaret. Happily the weather held good and did not prohibit the flight. On royal schedule the Princesses were in Lord Sefton's box immediately after the first race and presently walked down to the paddock with Lord Derby and Lord Sefton to see Monaveen paraded. Princess Elizabeth may well have felt that half the pleasure of racing lay in anticipation. Over the two miles seven furlongs of the shortened Aintree course, Monaveen jumped faultlessly and soared over the last fence still ahead of Freebooter. But then that fatal idiosyncrasy of finding no extra momentum for the last run-in drastically told, and it was Monaveen second, a place that nevertheless ensured a reasonable gain. No trace of the terrific emotional let-down of the last few moments showed as Princess Elizabeth gaily congratulated Mrs. Brotherton, the Yorkshire owner of the winner.

Nevertheless, Monaveen at that time remained the most popular horse in Britain. The growing possibility that he might achieve a royal Grand National engaged the national imagination. Tony Grantham already felt the horse might win over the longer course. Princess Elizabeth flew to Malta to spend her second wedding anniversary with her husband and was not present at Sandown Park to see Monaveen put at the fences on the difficult slopes in the Walton Green Handicap. His chief rival was Salmiana II and it might have been a close finish. The fighting mare was with him all the way, right to the last fence, where she blundered and fell. Then Tony Grantham merely had to take his horse ahead and he won by fifteen lengths.

The news was cabled to the Princess and she replied, congratulating the trainer and rider and confirming Monaveen's engagement in the Queen Elizabeth Handicap Chase, a new race inaugurated by the Hurst Park executive for the last day of the year. Her Royal Highness was amused to find that the Press was calling him 'The horse that wins blindfold', from the practice of running Monaveen in blinkers, originated when Monaveen showed too strong a tendency to look outside the wings when approaching his jumps. But his ability to win blindfold would have to be exceptional if he were to win against the formidable array of competitors at Hurst Park.

Nearly every steeplechasing champion in the country was in the field. There was the unimpeachable Freebooter — as if giving Monaveen a return match — Wot No Sun, and Lord Bicester's Roimond, a great broad-backed giant who would crash through fences and led many a race at a terrific gallop. The Princess must have noticed with some disquiet that he was second to Cottage Rake in the big race at Kempton Park on Boxing Day. Clearly the Queen Elizabeth Chase was not to be missed, and events happily fitted in. H.M.S. *Chequers* was due to sail on exercises in the Red Sea on December 28th. The Princess flew to London the following day, had a free day for accumulated correspondence and affairs at Clarence House and was at Hurst Park soon after lunch.

Both Mr. Cazalet and his rider were confident, although the three-mile race promised a ding-dong struggle with every chasing veteran in England. And so it proved. Roimond was in one of his surly, lagging moods but Wot No Sun commenced a stern struggle with Monaveen. First one, then the other, was in the lead, both sailing their fences imperturbably and a mile and a half had gone before Wot No Sun fell a length behind. Then Freebooter and Klaxton challenged strongly. Listening in at Sandringham, the Queen Mother must have sat on the edge of her chair. The Princess excitedly jumped up and down. Then Monaveen took his last fence alone.

The uproar of the crowd was truly phenomenal, for Monaveen had been freely offered at 10–1 by doubtful bookies and had been heavily backed. Nor was Monaveen's fatal flaw to mar that final run-in. For perhaps the first, but happily not the only, time in his career he decidedly accelerated after clearing the jump and won handsomely. The Princess beamed with joy as she went to the unsaddling enclosure to congratulate Tony Grantham and give her horse an approving pat. Mr. Cazalet, fully sharing her delight, came in for his full share of credit and thanks for the notable improvement in form. Her Royal Highness stayed to watch the next race when Lord Mildmay, who had been in the Royal Box, came in third. Then the Princess left for Sandringham to spend the last hours of the old year with the Royal Family, glowingly aware that Monaveen in the National assuredly loomed as one of the big racing events of 1950. Winning £2,300, he had more than doubled his initial purchase price. Moreover, the New Year was not long on its way when, as if to underline the tide in his affairs, Monaveen also won the George Williamson Handicap Chase by a length against five runners at Hurst Park, a race the Queen flew specially from Sandringham to see.

III

They were all there at Aintree — the King and Queen, the Princess Elizabeth, the Princess Margaret, and the Duchess of Kent. It was the first time the Sovereign had honoured the course with his presence since the days of George V. The royal train stood in the siding. Princess Margaret propitiously was about to embark on her first official tour of Lancashire and was spending the weekend at Knowsley Hall. But the Royal Family needed no excuse whatsoever for their attendance save the fun of the day. They were all as happy and expectant as children at a fête. Some sharp-eyed souls noticed that Princess Elizabeth was wearing her 'good luck' hat, and she had indeed chosen to wear the same hat she had selected for Monaveen's notable victory at Hurst Park. The day had dawned fine and the course glittered with sunshine. Mr. Cazalet reported that the royal horse had recovered from the journey and was in the pink of condition. Princess Elizabeth chatted with enthusiasm as the mammoth field of forty-nine paraded.

They were all there, too, Monaveen's greatest rivals, Freebooter and Wot No Sun; the previous year's winner, Russian Hero; the rugged Roimond, Cloncarrig, Tommy Traddles, Cottage Welcome, Cromwell, Zarter, and many more. Very small Monaveen looked alongside some of the giants, as if his burden of ten stone thirteen pounds might be excessive. The jockeys had found conditions in the early races perfect. For this year at least the mud or the visibility could never be blamed for a lapse. Yet still only the King looked anxious during those tense minutes while the starter assembled the unwieldy field and it was noticed that Princess Elizabeth spoke to him reassuringly. Then, with the great roar of Aintree, they were off!

The first 470 yards of flat always separates the horses, but a fair proportion, this time, were bunched at the first fence and, from the stands, men and horses seemed to hurtle in all directions. Russian Hero fell, Tommy Traddles crashed, but the cry was taken up from the rails to the stands, 'Monaveen's up!' and practically drowned the loudspeakers. At the second fence and the third fence, the commentator reported more tumbles and loose horses were careering in every direction.

But meanwhile Monaveen was in the lead at a fierce pace with Wot No Sun. The Princesses were both flushed with excitement. Both horses cleared the fourth and fifth fences; Wot No Sun had a slight lead, and the crowd quietened for news from Becher's Brook. Speed is the only hope here; both leaders took it like swallows, but for Monaveen the sight of the next fence ahead gave him a slight leading impetus, though he practically stood on his head on the turf. Roimond and Freebooter were at his heels. But within seconds Roimond fell at the seventh fence and was out of the race. Remember, each entrant in the National has already won a three-mile race worth at least £300, any chase worth £400 or has been placed at Aintree, guarantees of sheer stamina. Yet the field was stringing out while Monaveen was still leading, successfully negotiating the tricky left-hand Canal Turn, Valentine's Brook, and the three fences beyond. But as they came down towards the stands, Monaveen and Wot No Sun still duelling, the inexplicable happened. In many respects it was like the tragic halt of Devon Loch six years later. As he neared the wall of sound that greets a winning royal runner, he jibbed, thrusting back from the fourteenth fence so abruptly that Tony Grantham was all but unseated. He would indeed have been flung from the saddle if Arthur Thompson on Wot No Sun had not instantaneously impulsively flung out a steadying hand, pushing him back into balance.

Monaveen duly took the fence but he had lost five lengths. Cloncarrig was now ahead and the 33–1 Acthon Major coming up close. The Queen's, that is to say, the Princess Elizabeth's eager smile seemed to blaze an assurance that her horse could still recover the lead. He was safely over the treacherous Chair jump and the spectacular water jump, and had thus safely completed the first circuit of the course. Over half the field had fallen out and they dwindled to a handful at Becher's. Yet there still was Monaveen, tiring sufficiently for Freebooter to pass him by but still game and dogged. With only two fences left, Freebooter and Cloncarrig held the lead, with Monaveen still paired with Wot No Sun and Acthon Major at their heels. Then, at the last fence but one (the ominous thirteenth fence to superstitious riders on the first round) Cloncarrig stumbled, failed to right herself and went rolling.

It was Freebooter who streaked first past the winning-post, with Wot No Sun second, and then Acthon Major. The Duchess of Kent patted the Princess encouragingly on the arm, while the Queen looked at her consolingly. Princess Elizabeth shrugged her shoulders and smiled. Monaveen lay fifth but he had never derelicted from duty. All but seven horses had fallen. The result was disappointing but not disillusioning: a salutary reminder, perhaps, that even for a royal owner there may be horses better than one's own. Shaking hands yet again with Freebooter's owner, Mrs. Brotherton, Princess Elizabeth looked as if she really meant it when she remarked, cheerfully, 'I'm so glad — for you!' She learned with interest that

Freebooter had been bred on a Waterford farm and heard indeed that his full brother still pulled a plough.

There was always tomorrow and the Princess, it is said, seemed full of resolve to win a Grand National one day. Perhaps Monaveen could still make the attempt. In the one season in any event he had brought the partners £3,293 in four races. And so, before the King and Queen and Princess Elizabeth returned to London the following day, Mr. Cazalet had already been encouraged to lay further plans for Monaveen as well as to bear in mind the purchase of future steeplechasers.

IV

There were nevertheless sombre undertones that summer as Monaveen continued in training at Fairlawne. Early in May tragic news reached the stable when Lord Mildmay disappeared while bathing from a Devon beach and was later found drowned. He had been an enjoyable guest in the Royal Box at Aintree, and had genially squired the then Queen for Monaveen's George Williamson victory at Hurst Park. Barely six months earlier Princess Elizabeth had been a guest at his home while touring the West Country, and Princess Margaret attended her first National Hunt meeting in his company during a stay at Torpoint with the Carew Poles. The Royal Family mourned a close friend, and when Lord Mildmay's horses came up for disposal, the Queen decided to buy one of the most promising and continue his chasing career.

The horse honoured for this commemoration was Manicou, by the ominously named Last Post out of Mylae, whom Lord Mildmay had ridden to victory no less than six times in nine races during the last busy steeplechasing season of his life. With this exceptional novice was also purchased a promising three-year-old whom Mr. Cazalet had discovered in Ireland, a grey gelding by Owenstown out of Desla's Star whom the Queen named Killarney.

On August 10th, five days before the birth of Princess Anne, the Kang was in no mood for desk work and he and the Queen motored down to Tonbridge to see these purchases as well as to inspect Monaveen. The latter was in fine fettle, as well he might be for a horse who had won his young mistress £3,293 in four races, and Their Majesties discussed his future happily. The Grand Sefton Trial Chase, the Grand Sefton itself, as in 1949, and the Queen Elizabeth Chase were the preliminaries planned for another National. It had to be admitted that there were interesting new rivals in the field, including Coloured Schoolboy, a superb jumper successful in sixteen races, but one never could tell.

Princess Elizabeth was unable to see Monaveen's first run of the 1950-1 season in the Sefton Trial. The Duke of Edinburgh was flying home from Malta for Princess Anne's christening and Princess Elizabeth wished to meet him at London Airport, but the Queen Mother was at Hurst Park to give Tony Grantham her usual encouragement. Unhappily, there was no propitious success to report to her daughter, for Coloured Schoolboy won again. Monaveen was now too 'up in the weights'. The horse still flew at his fences like a bird and pleased his jockey. But in the Sefton he might have been the thirteenth guest in the field of thirteen. Among the runners were Freebooter, Shagreen, one of Ireland's best horses, Finnure, who had won the Champion Stakes, Russian Hero, and Acthon Major. The result was Shagreen's win, with Freebooter, Finnure, Russian Hero, and Monaveen trailing next, in that order.

The King and Queen had hoped to see Manicou carrying the Queen's colours for the first time on November 2nd, but the death of King Gustav of Sweden on October 29th imposed the protocol of Court mourning. Instead, Princess Elizabeth went to Fontwell, recalling all the beginner's excitement of her first day with Monaveen. The new colours of blue, buff stripes, and blue sleeves, with a black cap and gold tassel, were effective, but the Princess noticed alertly that the blue looked washed out. In keeping with this laundered hue, Manicou came in seventh in a very moderate field.

Would nothing halt the royal chasing hoodoo? Talking to the Duchess of Norfolk at Fontwell, the Princess discovered that the Arundel horse Possible was engaged in the Wimbledon Handicap Chase for which Manicou was also entered and it had to be remembered that Possible was a distinct possibility, all the more so within a few days when he won the Molyneux Chase at Aintree.

At all events, the Queen and Princess Elizabeth were both at Kempton Park three weeks later to see the Wimbledon Chase. Before the big race, Manicou's previous victorious opponent at Fontwell, Sir Sydney Palmer's Attentif, won an earlier handicap. The omen-wise thereupon had much to say of Manicou's bleak outlook, but racing proves time and again that nothing is more deceptive than its signs and portents. With Dick Francis on Possible and Tony Grantham on Manicou, a display of faultless riding was inevitable.

Incidentally, talking to Tony Grantham in the paddock, the Queen and Princess Elizabeth discussed his jacket and discovered why the blue seemed so pale. The colours had been exactly copied, too exactly copied, from a set fifty years old without making allowance for fading. A new set had been ordered.

Then the race began, in such perfect visibility that every moment of the three miles could be savoured and enjoyed. In less than a mile, both Manicou and Possible drew ahead of the leaders. Manicou's white blaze could be clearly seen. The two made the running all the way until Manicou jumped slightly ahead at the last fence and sprinted away on the flat to a first-class win. Possible was actually eight lengths behind.

The Queen and Princess Elizabeth were cheered handsomely as they made their way to the unsaddling enclosure, their radiant smiles revealing their intense pleasure. It was the first time a Queen had won in her own colours since the days of Queen Anne. One good day, a perfect day's racing at that, could remove all the nettle-stings of failure.

'Now it's Monaveen's turn,' said Princess Elizabeth.

It was, on the contrary, to be Manicou's turn, and it is fortunate that the Princess flew out to Malta at the end of November to be cushioned against the shock that lay in store, a shock she would otherwise have encountered at close hand. Her Royal Highness and her husband were to visit the King and Queen of the Hellenes, an engagement that controlled the tempo of events, for otherwise one imagines the Princess would not have missed the hoped-for spectacle of Monaveen possibly winning the Queen Elizabeth Chase for the second year running.

The Queen herself flew from Sandringham for the race. It was a dismal day of mud and swirling mist. The Queen's car indeed stuck slithering in the mud on leaving the Hurst Park gates and had to be pushed clear by racegoers, an indignity, so to speak, in woeful keeping with the afternoon. There were only nine runners in the main chase and Monaveen was with the leaders approaching the water-jump the second time round. Two other horses seemed to take the jump at the same time and Monaveen perhaps jumped a yard too soon. They were so close that some witnesses thought they saw a collision in mid-air.

Tony Grantham was convinced, afterwards, that there had not been a touch but everything happened so quickly. Monaveen came down off-balance and landed twisted, flinging the jockey over his neck before he fell heavily, struggled, and could not rise.

Mr. Cazalet ran across from the Stewards' Box where he had been watching with the Queen and returned sadly to say that Monaveen had broken a leg and would have to be shot. Tony Grantham had been knocked out in the fall but the ambulance men were bringing him round and could find no harm.

The Queen did not leave the course until she was reassured. She asked, too, if she could see the BBC commentator, Raymond Glendenning, whom Her Majesty knew had been broadcasting the race. To Mr. Glendenning she explained that she was certain the news would upset Princess Elizabeth, who was listening in Malta. But Mr. Glendenning was able to reassure her that the news had not been broadcast. He had been concentrating on the winner, Coloured Schoolboy.

The Queen was able to break the news gently in her own way by telephone. 'It's so sad, so terribly sad,' she said, before leaving the course. And later to the officials greeting her at London Airport she explained, 'It's been such a sad day.' And Monaveen now lies buried in a grave overlooking the racecourse where he died.

V

If horses were able to read the human heart, that great *if* of history, Manicou might have been expected to make up for Monaveen. He did his best the following week in the three-

and-a-half-mile Ewell Handicap Chase at Sandown Park when young Bryan Marshall rode him home first in a field of nine in the Queen's presence. Again at Kempton Park on Boxing Day he showed such a clean pair of heels in the three-mile run for the £2,100 King George VI Chase that Turf historians wrote approvingly, 'That day he could have beaten the best in the land.'

Many of the best were indeed represented, for the opposition included Coloured Schoolboy, the big chestnut Silver Fame, acknowledged the greatest horse Lord Bicester ever owned, Cobios, who had won a three-miler at Cheltenham, and Rhetorious, Manicou's French-bred stable companion. Once more the Queen was at Kempton Park, driving from Sandringham in bitter weather. Once more Her Majesty was able to telephone her daughter in Malta news of a superb race, for Manicou had jumped perfectly at every fence, with Marshall up. Then Silver Fame drew up to him at the very last fence. There they both were ... and Manicou sprinted away to win. It was a thrilling finish.

Yet an element of uncertainty which Manicou had evinced over the Fontwell hurdles was not unnatural in a full colt. Two months after his George VI triumph, Princess Elizabeth returned from Malta and accompanied her parents to Sandown to see him in the Annual Handicap Chase. He was far behind. Nor was he much better a week later when the Queen and the two Princesses went to Lingfield, though the day had its moments. The Royal Party were lustily cheered on arrival by a merry crowd of schoolgirls clustered at the gates of the racecourse. Enquiring where they were from, the Queen learned they came from a neighbouring convent!

Shortly afterwards, Manicou broke down and was retired to stud. Prepared to accept the pleasures of steeplechasing philosophically as they came, the Queen had in any event invested in another chaser. This was another Irish-bred five-year-old who had never produced a mark of any kind on racing records until he won a flat race for amateur riders over two miles at Naas. Once more Peter Cazalet acted quickly on recognizing quality and completed purchase for the Queen within a month.

The name of the unknown newcomer was Devon Loch.

7: ABOVE BOARD — SELSKAR ABBOT — REPRIMAND

I

One other horse considerably interested the Princess Elizabeth during those few happy, busy, domestic, and unalloyed years before she came to the Throne. This was Above Board, a filly foal of Feola's by Straight Deal, thus a half-sister of Hypericum and Angelola, born at Hampton Court in the year of the Princess's marriage. One detects the Duke of Edinburgh's dry humour in the name originally chosen, Overboard, a name properly jettisoned in due course. Here again was a foal to be watched from her first halting steps in the foaling-box, a foal with whom Prince Philip could photograph the Princess during one of those Corsham interludes. Straight Deal was, of course, Miss Dorothy Paget's 1943 Derby winner, a son of Solario–Good Deal who had proved himself the best stayer out of a field that included Persian Gulf, Umiddad, and Nasrullah. Here was good thoroughbred breeding and the Princess may have wondered, checking off Angelola's victory in the Yorkshire Oaks in 1948, whether the sister filly would not prove just as capable.

A film, which was naturally called *All the King's Horses* had been made at the Hampton paddocks, showing Feola and other residents and boarders, and Above Board made a brief but effective appearance, but few of the names of the younger stock will be remembered. Certainly a new deal was about due in the King's racing luck, for His Majesty's handsome 1948 prize total of £13,207 with thirteen wins was sharply halved in 1949 to £6,788 with only three wins. Avila's rich gain in the

Coronation Stakes at Ascot represented the bulk of this sum. In 1950 it stood at £8,750 for twelve races and would have been greatly diminished but for the sums Above Board salvaged in place-money and her supreme win of £3,310 in the Cesarewitch.

The 1948 two-year-olds from the National Stud which were intended to give a fillip to the 1949 season somehow went wrong — Gigantic achieved four places in his third year before retirement to stud; Berrylands went amiss after winning at Salisbury, and made no impression at Ascot. Royal Blue was, as Gordon Richards said, 'delightful to look at', but he held no wins. Retracing these pages of royal racing, we left Princess Elizabeth and her husband on a frosty January day, inspecting Astrakhan and the King's two-year-old Boyd-Rochfort string of 1949. Northern Light, Gaywood, Somerset House, Knight Commander, Hunting Song, Harriet, and Above Board: oddly enough, the throw-out Astrakhan made an ultimately better showing than most. In lieu of sterner stuff among the royal horses the Princess found herself keeping a friendly eye on Mr. Woodward's Boyd-Rochfort colt Prince Simon, and Mr. Winston Churchill's Colonist II, while of the Murless string Mrs. Macdonald-Buchanan's Abernant perhaps merited her attention.

Recovering from his leg operation, the King did not attend the 1949 Derby and in a sense the Princess Elizabeth was there as his deputy to see the sensational photo finish between Nimbus and Leon Volterra's Amour Drake. This was the race that M. Volterra, stricken with desperate illness, had hoped to win before he died. Madame Volterra listened-in to the race and then told him the news he most wanted to hear, that his horse had won. But Princess Elizabeth knew nothing of this drama as she joined in the tense wait with the crowd on what was to her undoubtedly the supreme issue of whether a French or a British horse had won. Avila unhappily ran only fifth in the Oaks the previous day but Edgar Britt alertly wrested victory for the Yorkshire horse, Musidora, from the French filly, Coronation V. Avila, however, redeemed herself by winning the Coronation Stakes at Royal Ascot before Princess Elizabeth and her mother and the King, who watched as much of the racing as he could while seated in an armchair.

The bookies, one remembers, raised a rumpus when they found they were expected to remove their stands and impedimenta from a space on Ascot Heath beyond the Royal Box. The police had formed a gap by erecting signs, 'No bookmakers beyond here'. Angrily the fraternity protested that they had used the ground for years, that they had staked a claim. But when a police inspector explained that the King could not stand for long, and that the gap gave him a better view of the racing, there was no argument. 'That's different,' said the ringleader. 'Double file, boys.' And the bookmakers sorted themselves out without further ado.

The gap was still there a month later, when the King and Queen, the Princesses, and the Duchess of Kent arrived unexpectedly and almost unnoticed for the start of the Red Oaks Stakes, to see Harry Carr finish third, and the Princesses walked down through the crowd to watch the horses in the paddock for the Queen Elizabeth Stakes, an enjoyable snatched racing afternoon.

II

Above Board did not race as a two-year-old, but she made her bow to the racing public at Epsom in mid-April 1950 in the Princess Elizabeth Stakes, a race for three-year-old fillies over a mile, and it must be said with regret that she was almost last in.

Yet strangely enough she was so improved for the Oaks Trials three weeks later that she came in second behind Stella Polaris and ahead of Sirocco at third place and Astrakhan fourth. It must have led to much family teasing when the King's horse was pitted against that of his daughter, particularly when Mr. Musker's Stella Polaris (who was to be third in the Oaks) proved at that time superior to both. Practically the full Royal Family mustered for the Oaks, The King and Queen, Queen Mary, Princess Elizabeth, Princess Margaret, the Princess Royal, and the Duke and Duchess of Gloucester, all were there. Unluckily their journey was not strictly necessary, for a Scotch mist veiled the course, cloaking horses and riders from time to time.

True to form, Above Board was not only behind Stella Polaris, who gained third place, but she also seemed to be outpaced by at least two other fillies, Sanlinea and Happy Haven, and a French demoiselle, La Baille. Instead of a royal win, M. Boussac took home the £13,000 prize with his mare Asmena, who hobbled down to the start as if lame and strongly reminded old-timers of the lameness Coronach evinced before his Derby. Moreover, on Derby Day, Princess Elizabeth saw the defeat to second place of her favoured Prince Simon, while M. Boussac won another £17,000 with Galcador.

'But what is your secret? There must be a secret and you must tell me,' the Queen said, in congratulating Madame Boussac.

'Is it not in blending the best blood lines and finding just the right outcrossings?' Princess Elizabeth suggested, a formula to which, in fact, M. Boussac admitted at the Gimcrack dinner later that year.

Although the first royal win of the season was with Northern Hope, a Boyd-Rochfort two-year-old, in a race at Leicester, the fondness for Above Board nevertheless persisted. She was indeed to justify all their hopes, though taking her time. Royal Ascot came round again, and Princess Elizabeth evidently persuaded her parents to visit the course with her the day beforehand, a slight departure from tradition. Enormous changes were going on in landscaping the Royal Family's own racecourse: it was as if a private family were inspecting their garden the day before opening it to the public. The Princess noticed that the great gates needed regilding, perhaps even replacing, and there was the premises of the Windsor Forest stud, newly acquired as stabling, to inspect and discuss. Even the Royal Family that year could not be sure it would not be another French Ascot. The French had twenty-one runners. As it turned out, only one achieved a win, namely, Fastlad in the Gold Vase.

Princess Elizabeth was not in the royal procession that year, preferring to arrive privately by car with Sharman Douglas, and it was not until the second day that Above Board ran in the Ribblesdale Stakes. Once again the extraordinary form comparisons of Stella Polaris and the royal filly rang true, for Stella Polaris came in fourth, with Above Board immediately behind her, fifth, and the improving French-bred La Baille won. Then there was the excitement of Colonist II's struggle for the Gold Cup, and although Mr. Churchill's horse was fourth in a field of thirteen, the Cup was preserved for England by Mr. Wilfrid Harvey's Supertello, admirably jockeyed by Doug Smith. Altogether, Princess Elizabeth enjoyed herself so much that, flinging Queen Victoria's dictum to the winds, she arrived on the course for the 'Heath' meeting on the Saturday, enjoying the pageantry of the meeting, with

Princess Margaret, long before racing began. The King and Queen did not join them until the third race.

III

Looking back at 1950, a summer made memorable in any case by the advent of Princess Anne, our beloved present Queen must gratefully remember the happiness of many racing pleasantries with her father. The year that began with the National Hunt excitements of Monaveen continued with the happy fulfilments of Astrakhan and the growing anticipations of Above Board. The trend of royal racing, often as variable as the weather, set fair in July when the King scored a double at Nottingham one afternoon with his two-year-olds, Northern Hope and Nor'wester, both daughters of Borealis and both ridden by Carr. Freemason Lodge was clearly turning them out again. And precisely a week after the arrival of Princess Anne on August 15th Above Board commemorated the occasion by winning the Yorkshire Oaks, and some £1,800 for the King's purse, against Gordon Richards on Plume II and Rae Johnstone on Corejada. No wonder Eph Smith was still smiling to himself as he unsaddled, having ridden his first winner for the King.

Naturally, there were immense hopes for Above Board, too, in the Park Hill Stakes at Doncaster and the Princess Royal Stakes at Ascot. Barely a fortnight divided these races. With maddening persistency, Smirke on La Baille won the Park Hill, with Stella Polaris second, and Above Board came fourth after a prolonged struggle with Morning Madame. In the Princess Royal Stakes there were only six runners over the one and a half miles and Gordon Richards rode Plume II first past the post, with Carr on Above Board second, and Smirke on Stella Polaris third. There were sighs of relief at the transposition, at

96

long last, of Above Board and the redoubtable filly she had shadowed all season.

Now the stage was set for new ventures. The intention had been to try for the Newmarket Oaks, but Eph Smith, riding 'A.B.' in her gallops, kept cheerfully insisting she could do better. He was convinced she could win the Cesarewitch, and Eph had sound reason for judgment, for he had already won the Cesarewitch twice. Captain Boyd-Rochfort had to weigh his jockey's eagerness for a hat-trick — and indeed his own — against a dozen other considerations. A Cesarewitch winner must be endowed with sufficient stamina to win over the steep distance of two miles two furlongs, and in thirty years only three fillies had been able to fulfil this demand. The handicaps, moreover, induce unfamiliar and exacting values. Yet the King was agreeable to the entry and regarded it with some relish. Above Board was the only horse in the stable able to gallop with Prince Simon and her outings had been progressive. 'I don't think the Cesarewitch will take much winning this year,' Captain Boyd-Rochfort summed up with some dryness after he had studied one of the largest entry lists ever known.

Captain Moore and the trainer conferred and came to a decision only the weekend before the race. It was all settled so quickly that neither the King, who had arranged a shooting party that day, nor Princess Elizabeth could be present, and the Princess Royal was the only member of the Royal Family who attended the race. Captain Boyd-Rochfort estimated with complete accuracy that the horse would be carrying seven stone ten pounds, but he could not have anticipated such a runaway victory. The Cesarewitch is always Newmarket's greatest scramble and the field of thirty-eight that year was a record. But Eph Smith was not content to face a show of hooves.

Above Board strode to the lead a quarter-mile out, and kept it up. There was soon an ever-widening gap and gratified racegoers were soon able to shout their heads off, for Above Board won unchallenged by six lengths. In the final stages, it was a one-horse race and Above Board finished still full of running and on a tight rein. She had won her niche in racing history as the best-staying filly then in training, and of all the choice Boyd-Rochfort horses she was the first to get the Cesarewitch since his Seminole and Enfield in 1933 and 1934. Naturally, she was to be kept on as a four-year-old. The King's twelve winners of 1950 brought him £8,850 to which Above Board was the principal contributor. In 1951 the King's ten wins brought £4,724. But it must be added that Above Board's quota proved not so conspicuous as had been hoped.

A minor crisis arose when Mr. Woodward decided to return his horse, Prince Simon, to America. P.S. and A.B., as some of the hands called them, had become such good pacemakers to one another. If the filly was to be prepared for the Ascot Gold Cup, she needed a partner of equal mettle. For a few days that autumn Above Board was stabled at Wolferton for the King's inspection, and Princess Elizabeth did not omit to pay the filly an admiring visit, while also bidding farewell to Northern Light, who was to be sold. In eight races Northern Light had won only one, a small affair at Thirsk. Meanwhile the King had also bought Selskar Abbot, a beautiful brown colt by Remember II–June Baby who had won the Chippenham Stakes and seemed just the right lead for Above Board. The odd point is that Selskar Abbot distinguished himself almost as much in his fourth year as the champion horse for whom he had entered royal service.

IV

The pages turn to the Whit Monday meeting at Hurst Park, when both Princess Elizabeth and Sir Winston Churchill lunched with the stewards before watching the racing together, and the King and the great statesman were racing rivals in the Winston Churchill Stakes. An enormous crowd, lured by a mixed programme of flat-racing and National Hunt events, gave both Princess and politician a rousing welcome. Sir Winston was in his most jovial mood, pleased with his companion and beaming at the symptoms of popularity. As Joseph Garrity has said, he had only to set foot on a racecourse to transform the proceedings into a delirious V-Day in miniature. Racing with him, in his father's pink-and-chocolate colours, was still a fresh and novel preoccupation and his horse, Colonist II, with some sixth wins and a fourth place in the 1950 Gold Cup, sufficiently evinced the Churchill spirit.

It was amusing now to be pitting his own horse against that of his Sovereign, not without chuckling grumbles at the uneven odds, for the King was running both Above Board and Selskar Abbot. The Princess, to whom he had been a formidable and venerable figure for so long, enjoyed discussing thoroughbreds with him, and had been full of appreciation for Colonist II ever since his early win of the Lime Tree Stakes. In the Churchill Stakes, it turned out, Colonist II and Above Board were the only two horses of consequence, the crowds equally divided in deciding whether to follow 'Winnie' or the King. After a neck-and-neck run, Colonist won by two lengths from Above Board, with Star-Spangled Banner straggling third and Selskar coming fifth.

The Princess's smiling response to defeat was to invite a return match. Two weeks later the issue was re-tried over the same course in the White Rose Stakes. Yet the result was decisive. This time Mrs. Lilley's Pan II, who had won the 1950

Gold Cup from Colonist, was entered: and it was Colonist first, Pan II second, and Above Board third.

The King, constantly in the hands of the doctors, had not been at Epsom for the Derby and was absent from Ascot. In the middle of Ascot week a medical bulletin announced that a prolonged convalescence was essential, and the anxieties of the Queen and the Princesses, racegoing more for the duty of traditional ritual than enjoyment that year, seemed curiously matched in the races. The columnists were arguing that England's main hope of winning the 1951 Gold Cup was with Above Board, although they admitted she did not seem good enough. Though Colonist II was giving battle again, he, too, seemed outclassed. In the end it was Pan II first, with the French-trained Alizier second, and Above Board third. But it did not seem to matter.

Captain Boyd-Rochfort had to report that Selskar Abbot was ill with stomach trouble, and it may be characteristically true that the King joked, 'My horse and I are a pair.' But his spirits were dampened when Selskar was found dead in his box one morning, having had a heart attack in the night. Just to cap this Above Board was defeated to fifth in the July Stayer's Stakes at Sandown, her final appearance before retirement to stud. It was, of course, Friday the thirteenth.

More happily, the King was able to watch the Queen and Princess Elizabeth by television during their visit to the July Ascot Meeting for the rich Festival Stakes. The Queen Elizabeth Stakes and George VI Stakes were combined for the first time that year, creating a prize of £25,172 plus a commemorative piece of plate for the King and Queen. Colonist was there again, but it was feared that continental horses would scoop the kitty, and Princess Elizabeth's smile was specially bright when practically the only colt of pure

English thoroughbred stock, Mrs. Lilley's Supreme Court, saved the day and streaked first home.

The King's personal racing string that year was smaller than average. Apart from Selskar and Above Board, the interest of father and daughter centred mainly on the two-year-olds at Freemason Lodge; on Stream of Light, by Borealis–Yeovil; on Choir Boy, the son of Hyperion out of Captain Moore's Choral; on Prescription, by Epigram–Hypericum, and on Battered Down, the scion of Ocean Swell and Open Warfare. Of the National Stud horses, Deuce, son of Dante, seemed to promise best. He had been beaten only by inches at Goodwood and had the misfortune to tie in a Doncaster race and then lose it in the draw. In addition, the King had another of Feola's offspring, Reprimand by Court Martial, in training with Captain Charles Elsey in Yorkshire.

Princess Elizabeth put these racing interests to good purpose in attempting to cheer and encourage her father along the slow road of hoped-for recovery that followed his lung operation on September 23rd. Instead of leaving by sea two days later for their Canadian tour as planned, the Princess and her husband arranged to fly on October 7th, leaving a dozen free days on their hands. On September 27th the Princess visited Ascot to see Windsor Forest making his debut in the Clarence House Stakes. Though he was never conspicuous, it helped no doubt to make news to interest Papa. Next day Princess Margaret was encouraged to go to the races with her sister, and on October 4th the King had four runners at Newmarket.

Windsor Forest was entered for the two o'clock only to finish seventh behind a horse named Stone of Destiny. Choir Boy and Deuce had an outing together in the National Foal Stakes and though Gordon Richards rode Deuce to victory, Choir Boy was miserably nowhere. An attempt by Reprimand in the Bentinck Nursery Stakes rounded off the day. Then, on October 12th, when Princess Elizabeth telephoned her mother across the Atlantic, it was to hear that Choir Boy had finished fifth in a comparatively big field in the Sandwich Stakes. The little colt was improving. Racing was also a topic a day or two later when the Princess heard that her father had spent a happy afternoon watching the Ascot races by television.

The BBC had planned to start their commentary at 2.45, but the engineers were told that His Majesty could watch the running of his horse Good Shot in the Tankerville Nursery Stakes if the cameras could go into action a little earlier. So the King watched his Murless-trained protégé from his bed and, to his great satisfaction, saw a win. Gordon Richards positively flew out of the gate on Good Shot and rode one of his most skilful races to finish half a length ahead. The televised programme ran on until 4.10 enabling the King to watch the three runners of the Cumberland Lodge and the only two runners of the Diadem Stakes, an exciting duel between Royal Serenade and Mr. Ley On's 2,000 Guineas winner, Ki Ming, which the latter won.

Finally, on October 30th, Choir Boy achieved place honours in the Quy Stakes at Newmarket, coming third behind Agate and Tobias, and his owner may well have pondered his three-year-old prospects. But this was a season the King was sadly destined not to see.

Turned out smartly by Captain Elsey, Reprimand next appeared on November 8th at Liverpool and readily won the Seaboard Stakes. Princess Elizabeth was still in Canada. This was the last week but one of the flat-racing season and the last racing win of King George VI's life.

8: THE QUEEN'S ENTHUSIASM

I

In her twenty-sixth year, the historic year of her accession to the Throne, the Queen was no longer an initiate of the Turf but probably knew more about horses and horse-racing than any other young woman of her age in the world. This is by no means an exaggeration. Her Trooping the Colour appearance on Foxhunter's half-brother, the police horse Winston, had proved her as graceful and correct an exponent of equitation as the best riders in the land. And though Her Majesty had so far owned only one winner on the flat, she had versed herself intensively in thoroughbred breeding and stud management.

Her knowledge of pedigrees and breeding records, while not as absurdly encyclopaedic as some commentators imagine, was comprehensive and firmly grounded. Though only in her mid-twenties, she could talk of horses with such profound experts as the Aga Khan or Sir Humphrey de Trafford or the Duke of Beaufort on more than the common plane of enthusiasm. Behind her smiling, eager questions and outward diffidence there could already be detected a quiet authority and an inward fund of expertise that was at times almost professional.

Once, when inspecting a new horse which she thought of purchasing, she watched him trotting for a minute or two and then drew the veterinary surgeon's attention to the animal's breathing. 'Many members of my profession would envy Her Majesty's hearing,' the veterinary surgeon said afterwards. 'The sound the horse was making would have meant nothing except to an expert. But the Queen was right.'

On another occasion the Queen asked the specialist to examine a favourite hack. At first sight there was nothing wrong and normal clinical inspection found nothing amiss. Nevertheless, fuller diagnostic examination disclosed preliminary symptoms which fully confirmed the Queen's doubts. But for this thorough check the horse would have become dangerous to ride.

As a former riding master has pointed out, the Queen likes to apply herself without stint to every interest she takes up. One Christmas, escorted behind the scenes of the big circus at Olympia, she astonished the sons of the circus owner by identifying every breed of horses they had in the stables except one. The mystifying exception was a pair of black Friesians, a Dutch breed seldom seen in Britain outside the sawdust ring.

In the year before she succeeded to the Throne, too, the Queen, then Princess Elizabeth, watched one of the least anticipated finishes of the Derby. The favourite, Ki Ming, was being loudly cheered at the top of the hill when from the mass of bunched horses there spurted three outsiders, and at odds of 28–1 Mr. Joseph McGrath's Arctic Prince scored an overwhelming triumph of six lengths. Nearly everyone on the course was stupefied. The winning trainer, Mr. Stephenson, had never before run a horse in the Derby. The winning jockey, Spares, had never before had a Derby mount. Mr. McGrath, at one time one of the leaders of the Republican Army, did not mind admitting that he had been arrested with the Sinn Feiners and had spent some two years in Britain's gaols. It created a piquant situation when he was summoned to the Royal Box, but Mr. McGrath there met at least one person to whom the winner was not entirely unforeseen. With a twinkle in her eye, the then Princess Elizabeth showed him the speculative tick she had entered against Arctic Prince's name on her race-card. One could be wise after the event, knowing that Prince Chevalier was the sire, out of Arctic Sun, a daughter of Nearco. But the Princess knew also that Arctic Prince descended from St. Simon, and smilingly mentioned a royal ancestor in Persimmon. Although Mr. McGrath was also presented to Queen Mary and Princess Margaret, neither could obviously greet his success with such close insight as Princess Elizabeth eagerly showed and he left the Royal Box deeply impressed and, as he said, amazed at her bloodstock knowledge.

Yet in perspective it is not surprising that the Queen displays such a keen aptitude and has such an enthusiastic love of racing and bloodstock breeding. It would be surprising if it were not the case. British royal patronage had helped to make horse-racing the sport of kings. The Queen had long been trained as Heiress-Apparent, but she was also the eldest daughter of one of Britain's leading racing families. If one may venture into private terms, the family owned a world-famous racecourse as well as a racing string and two flourishing stud farms. And for the better part of a century, one or other of the studs, at Sandringham or Hampton Court, had exercised an immensely beneficial influence on racing stock throughout the world.

One of the Aga Khan's greatest brood mares stemmed from Memoir, an Oaks and St. Leger winner from the Royal Stud. A Hampton colt named Cambuscan, sold at the royal yearling auctions for forty guineas, afterwards changed hands for 4,000 guineas and was exported to Hungary, where he sired Kincsem, a subsequent winner of fifty-four races on the Austrian turf. In their Victorian heyday the royal paddocks maintained a hundred brood mares. Since the Second World War, more than sixty Hampton Court fillies have gone abroad, to win classic races in Canada, Australia, New Zealand, India, and the Argentine and afterwards to enrich the bloodstock strains of their new countries, immeasurably enhancing the prestige that the British bloodstock industry enjoys throughout the world. Is it surprising if the heiress of this profitable and long-established business should find horse-racing and breeding one of the engrossing hobbies of her extremely busy life?

One is conscious of charges, levelled among other outspoken and ill-founded attacks on the Queen, that her great love of horses amounts to an obsession. It is as well not to ignore these strictures, even though the Queen's public racegoing has been found to number not a dozen occasions in a year otherwise crammed with between 400 and 450 public engagements. If one may respectfully venture, then, to probe this so-called obsession in the manner of the psychiatrist, it is to find that in the Freudian terms of psychoanalysis, the horse is the symbol of heroic deeds.

If this is the accepted case for ordinary mortals, how much more for the Queen, born to murmur the solemn vows of the Coronation oath, destined to follow in the tradition of the kings and queens of history, wrought by a thousand influences to undertake heroic deeds disguised in royal discipline stimulated on nearly every occasion of pageantry by the tattoo of hooves ... and indeed taken to Westminster Abbey by the great team of processional horses in their ornate ceremonial harness drawing the Gold State Coach! How much more for her, taken as a child by her patriarchal grandfather to gaze up at the great bay withers of his favourite horse, or wandering under the arch of Egerton House where the names of the racewinners gleamed in gold!

Behind the Queen, indeed, there lies more than sixty potent years of family racing, and it is doubly interesting to weigh the comparisons so often made between the Queen and her great-grandfather, King Edward VII. Despite his racing companions, Edward did not enter flat-racing until he was forty-five and had two sons in their twenties. His first horse under Jockey Club rules promptly won a Maiden Plate, but subsequently toppled dead under the Prince's eyes on the vanished Stockbridge course and was found to have had heart disease. One cannot imagine our present Queen acquiring such a horse, let alone racing her, and as late as 1893, when 'Teddy' was in his urbane fifties, Richard Marsh gazed with dismay at the first eight royal horses entering his stables for training. The only two races they ever won reminded Marsh to the end of his days, as he said, that the greatest care, patience, and skill could not avail 'if horses be really bad and devoid of racing merit'.

It was Marsh's experience that Edward VII genuinely loved his horses, and looked forward to visiting them after divine service on a Sunday, but was not a highly competent judge. It was not until 1895 that the brother colts, Florizel II and Persimmon, improved his racing luck, soundly established when Persimmon won the 1896 Derby (after mulishly refusing to enter his box) and then the St. Leger and the following Gold Cup. It is said that Queen Victoria sent the first congratulatory telegram after Persimmon's Derby and quietly consented to visit Ascot if Persimmon were sure to win. The trainer could give no such reassurance and the Queen decided she could not witness a royal defeat.

A further full brother to Persimmon, Diamond Jubilee, capped Edward's final year as Prince of Wales by winning the Triple Crown — the 2,000 Guineas, the Derby, and St. Leger.

But he was a mettlesome giant, apt to lash out and kick anyone within reach and would even nastily attempt to bite his jockey's feet. 'I'm afraid he's a bad case,' said the Prince, after a particularly bad display when he had hurled his jockey through the air and dashed riderless up the Newmarket course, and Marsh had to beg to be allowed to keep him in training. When Diamond Jubilee appeared as a three-year-old, 'made no attempt to eat the bystanders' and won the second royal Derby, the Prince must have felt that all things were possible. Sending a £1,000 cheque as the Prince's present to Marsh, Lord Marcus Beresford conveyed the message, 'I hope you will win the Derby very often again for Sandringham.'

It was not, of course, until Minoru's Derby in 1909 that a major royal victory again delighted the nation. In his fourth year Diamond Jubilee bit off a stable-lad's finger and Marsh could not approach him in the box without risk of being savaged. No horse plainer indicated the time for retirement. Though King Edward VII hoped for 'reliable ones' to take his place, the King won only seven races during his first three years on the Throne. Chatsworth improved the record to five wins in 1904, two in 1905, and four in 1906. Yet the retired stallions, including Florizel II, Persimmon, and Diamond Jubilee, earned over a quarter-million pounds in fees. Princesse de Galles proved a good two-year-old filly, achieving four of the King's nine race wins in 1908. But it was not until Minoru came from Ireland, pliable clay in his trainer's hands after merely one two-year-old win, that King Edward's legendary success as a racehorse owner was even remotely justified during his reign.

Minoru was leased from the noted Tully stud, the establishment which a dozen years later was offered to the nation to become the basis of the National Stud. With a corky demeanour, the little bay seemed a certainty once he had won the 2,000 Guineas, and he entered the Derby as second favourite to win by a short head. There was an awful pause while the judges conferred. Then the number went up and a surging excited crowd swept jockey and horse across the course. Police and ropes were equally swept away as the King tried to reach the enclosure, swiftly surrounded by the dense throng, moving one step at a time and calmly saying in his guttural voice, 'Make way for the King!' A music-hall singer began singing 'God Save the King'. The anthem was taken up, swelling over Epsom Downs, while people wept with pleasure and emotion.

Minoru was afterwards exported to Russia and his fate remains unknown, but he was a forbear of the great Hyperion and thus of many horses inscribed in the General Stud Book of today. And of the thousands who cheered the King not one man could have guessed that he would be dead within three weeks of another Derby Day. The King's pleasure in his dying hours at hearing of the victory of one of his horses, Witch of the Air, at Kempton Park has been often told. Less sufficiently stressed is the fact that, of twenty-two horses in training, Witch of the Air provided his only racing triumph of the year.

King George V, too, had to wait a year for his first racing win. Until he ascended the Throne, his father had consistently discouraged him from owning racehorses but the racing fraternity soon found him a better judge of a horse even though his entries only once achieved a classic win, the 1928 1,000 Guineas. With the advantage of reading his diaries, his biographer, John Gore, found that he was never happier than in his rooms at Newmarket or among his yearlings and mares at Sandringham.

King George V always liked to be kept closely informed of progress, plans, and hopes, and was both grateful and delighted when he won. 'Never hurry a horse for me,' he observed to his trainer. 'When you tell me it is ready to run I shall be quite satisfied. I would much sooner have a nice three-year-old than a two-year-old.'

His worst racing disappointment was the 1924 Derby when his horse Knight of the Garter was well fancied but contracted heel-bug on the very eve of the race. In 1923, his best year, he had no fewer than nineteen wins. Betting in moderation, he also liked to think that he subsidized his stamp collection by the fruits of his knowledge of form. The accountancy of betting, however, puzzled him. In this, he differed from his father, who opened an account for £1,000 at Weatherby's and at one time had £60,000 to his credit.

The less desirable connotations that somehow still cling to the memories of King Edward VII's racegoing derive in reality from the unsavoury racing companions of his youth. It is of interest to contrast them with the irreproachable friends and companions with whom the Queen enjoyed discussing racing shop. Sir Harold and Lady Zia Wernher, their daughters, Mrs. Harold Phillips and Mrs. David Butter; the Duke and Duchess of Norfolk, the Duke and Duchess of Richmond and Gordon and the Duke and Duchess of Devonshire were among those notably privileged in this regard. In addition, the list of Ascot week house-party guests at Windsor, though purely social, will afford a reliable index for historians of the men and women honoured to share the enthusiasms of the Queen.

III

Tracing the family influences and the powerful, often unconscious, psychological factors that motivate the Queen's deep interest in racing, future biographers will unravel a complex mesh of reasons that underlie Her Majesty's enjoyment of her favourite recreation. Sir Gordon Richards put it simply, 'The Queen's obvious enjoyment ... has meant that there is an even closer connection between the Sovereign and the millions of her loyal subjects who agree with her that a day's racing is an absorbing way of temporarily relaxing from the worries of a very busy life, and therefore a grand way of freshening up from work done and for work to come.' Apart from the infinite pleasure and satisfaction that the ownership of fine horses afforded him, King Edward VII asserted forthrightly that racegoing enabled him to let off steam. His grandson, Edward VIII, echoed these words when he gave up steeplechasing, 'I reluctantly abandoned the one pursuit which gave outlet to my competitive spirit.' In the same way, enveloped in the cotton-wool of pomp and steeped continually in a hothouse atmosphere of reverence and adulation, the Queen in turn finds that her racing interests provide the great safety-valve.

Working at her boxes, the Queen never allows herself to feel suffocated or imprisoned by the immense strain and intense restrictions of her position. She has read and re-read a summary of the monarchy, in her possession, which was once drawn up by George V: 'The value of the Crown in its dignified capacity (*a*) It makes Government intelligible to the masses (*b*) It makes Government interesting to the masses... The moral value of the Crown. Great for good or evil.' And so forth. Constitutionally, it has been said, the Queen rules but has no voice of her own. The royal Prerogative includes the Right to Warn, the Right to be Consulted, yet the Sovereign can take no action except on advice. We prohibit the Queen from taking part in politics and exempt her from domestic affairs. Yet racing offers a vast untrammelled realm in which she can act as a free being, make up her own mind, form her own judgments, and act on them.

There is a special satisfaction in achieving distinction in such a hobby, in attempting to enhance the prestige of British bloodstock with new patterns, in watching race by race the fulfilment or obliteration of one's hopes. With the same pertinacious memory that George V devoted to philately, the Queen remembers when and where each of her horses won, what weight it was carrying and, as a term of reference, even the odds. As I have said, the Queen does not bet nor place wagers through her friends. An erring columnist who once said otherwise was instantly rebuked. Thus Her Majesty forestalls the captious plaints of those who might accuse her of supporting the more vicious side of gambling, with all the misery it supposedly invokes.

. Foal, winner, stud — it is with this recurrent cycle of the vast and valuable British bloodstock industry that the Queen is most concerned. She decides the breeding policy of her brood mares with a great deal of thought and care, fully discussing the choice of sires with Captain Moore, eagerly visiting the foals and often making shrewd suggestions later on when it comes to selecting races. Her racing manager and trainers may proffer advice, but the Queen gives the final directives which, with her planning team, have enhanced the worldwide reputation of Hampton Court in her reign.

All the royal yearlings go into training, for instance, but each year Her Majesty decides there are some she does not wish to keep and these are then sold privately, although the Queen still takes a close interest in their future. Foals are never sold and the output in quantity of the Royal Yearling Sales of Queen Victoria's era seems never likely to be reached in the present reign. The Queen breeds to race, although Queen Victoria bred to sell. The Royal Stud is nevertheless a source of some private profit, compensating Her Majesty to some slight extent for the extraordinary paucity of the Civil List, the royal allowance from the State. This has remained unchanged since 1952 despite the enormous drop in the purchasing value of the pound and has indeed increased only by a meagre £5,000 since Edwardian times.

9: CHOIR BOY AND GAY TIME

I

When the Queen succeeded to the Throne and thus found herself mistress overnight of the prized royal racing string, it was some time before she could bring herself to assess her new possessions. Barely three weeks before the King died, she had been enjoying the racing at Hurst Park with her mother but now all was changed. Roused from his sleep in New York to be told of the Sandringham tragedy, Captain Boyd-Rochfort said that he did not know what would happen. This guarded statement was instantly misinterpreted. In some quarters absurd quibbles were expressed of the propriety of the Queen owning racehorses. But the Queen early allayed anxiety in her racing establishments and elsewhere with the reassuring announcement that she would race on exactly the same lines as her father and that during the period of Court mourning her horses would carry the colours of the Duke of Norfolk.

The cancellation of royal racing plans would have caused widespread loss and even hardship, and this arrangement improved on the precedent of George V's accession when the King's horses were raced in his first season under lease to the Earl of Derby. Meanwhile, the Queen had nine racehorses in training with Captain Boyd-Rochfort and five under National Stud lease with Noel Murless. Of the former, the trainer's reports on Prescription and Battened Down were such that their future races were vetoed and the only remaining home-bred three-year-olds were Choir Boy and Stream of Light.

The two-year-olds included Double Entry, Windsor Forest, and a certain Aureole. Of the yearlings, the brightest hopes

114

were held for Festival Light, a filly by Rising Light–Feola and Angel Bright, by Hyperion–Angelola, Aureole's full sister. Of the shaggy brood mares, munching their hay, corn, and chaff at Hampton Court, much was awaited. King George VI had indulgently allowed his daughter to plan their engagements and the anticipated foals included offspring to Hypericum by Donatello II and to Astrakhan by Kingstone. The latter stallion was still earning his regularly advertised £98 fees at Wolferton.

None of the horses with Mr. Murless had ever raced, and towards the end of April the Queen took her mother to Beckhampton on the pretext of inspecting them. It was one of those considerate excursions necessary in bereavement. The Queen and the Queen Mother lunched with Mr. and Mrs. Murless and then saw three-year-old Ardent and his two-year juniors, Black Bee, Snow Princess, High Service, and Infernal Machine, put through a brisk gallop. Genially the Queen agreed that three of them deserved a prompt showing. Two of the Boyd-Rochfort string were also due, and so it came about that in the week of May 12th the Queen had five runners.

They were all raced in camera, so to speak, in the Duke of Norfolk's sky-blue with quartered cap. Infernal Machine did not get very far in the Lady Godiva Plate at Birmingham. High Service, Hyperion's daughter, vainly attempted the Wray Plate at Lingfield. Choir Boy had fluked his chance at Newbury on May 2nd when he failed to pass Sir Phoenix in the Rayner Stakes but he improved with eleven days' respite, and Harry Carr rode him home to victory over the Rowley Mile in the Wilberton Handicap on May 13th.

The wild cheer that went up from the initiated puzzled those unaware of the significance of the Norfolk colours. Some explained it indeed not as the Queen's first success but as the second Boyd-Rochfort win of the afternoon. Another royal horse, Long Range, missed his opportunity of creating a Newmarket double in the Pampisford Stakes. Ardent was equally an also-ran at Bath the following day. But she made amends, albeit still in Norfolk disguise, when Gordon Richards rode her to win by four lengths in the Rous Plate at Chepstow early in June. This can be counted the Queen's first honour for the National Stud. Meantime Stream of Light romped home under ducal sky-blue silk in the Katherine Parr Stakes at Hurst Park, the Duke of Norfolk's third and final obliging win as nominee.

The Queen did not visit Epsom for the Derby that year — the Royal Box remained closely curtained — and so Her Majesty missed the remarkable tantrums of Gay Time, who was shortly to become the first horse for whom she ever initiated a lease. The colt, one of six horses bequeathed to Mrs. J. V. Rank by her husband, put up a remarkable race and came in second three-quarters of a length behind the Aga Khan's Tulyar. He was no sooner past the finishing post, however, than he threw Lester Piggott and headed towards Epsom.

Could Gay Time have won? He was still going nicely when captured by a stable-boy a mile away and he had already recovered from a chapter of misadventure. First he cast a shoe in the parade ring and a farrier had to run to his aid. Then another shoe came loose and was hanging off at the post. Above all, Lester Piggott declared he was struck but after discussion it was decided not to object.

The huge field of thirty-three had been an exceptional scrimmage of men and horses. Billy Nevett on Torcross was nearly brought down and found his right leg thrown over another horse. A French jockey received a black eye, and one of the Boussac runners broke a fetlock and had to be shot. The Queen watched some slow-motion sequences in the Derby film she afterwards saw at Clarence House, but it was impossible to say who had knocked who. At all events, Tulyar was later sold to the Eire Government for £250,000 and the National Stud committee may have felt they were securing a bargain when, prior to this, they purchased Gay Time for £50,000. There were to be regrets, as we shall see.

II

Court mourning ended on May 31st, and it was announced the following week that the Queen's racehorses would run in her own name and colours, the adopted colours of the late King, purple, gold braid, scarlet sleeves, and black velvet cap with gold fringe. The Queen impulsively hoped to see Windsor Forest wearing her colours for the first time at Sandown Park but it was not to be. Harry Carr, it was felt, should have the prior engagement on Stream of Light in the Lancashire Oaks at Manchester. The problem of a rider for Windsor Forest was, however, solved with typical royal kindness and consideration.

The Queen proposed that the mount — and it was in reality an opportunity to achieve an historic win in her colours — should go to a young apprentice whom she had noticed at Arundel, named Freddy Durr. Poor Durr gamely did his utmost but the task was hopeless and his mount was to blame. Batstone, a sixteen-year-old apprentice, who was similarly given the horse, as his first mount at Nottingham the following month did very well to pull him in third. Windsor Forest lost six races before he won his seventh at Leicester under Carr's mastery, and the Queen thought it a very fair price when the colt was sold to a Scottish trainer later that season for 960 guineas.

Meanwhile, on that fateful June 7th, Carr found himself against tough opposition with Douglas Smith on Lord Derby's

Hortentia, who had been the runner-up rival in the Katherine Parr. Neck and neck the fillies raced, with Smith putting in a terrific challenge halfway up the finishing straight. The mighty roar of Northern racegoers when Stream of Light won the Queen's first racing victory in her own name and colours was indeed impressive.

In that first racing season, when the dark clouds receded and the Coronation plans began taking shape, events gaily quickened. The week after her first win, the Queen had another two runners at Brighton, when Gordon Richards won the Whitehawk Plate on Infernal Machine while Black Bee took a second in the Patcham Plate. Then came Royal Ascot, erroneously forecast as a black-and-white Ascot, the brilliant, bold, glittering first Ascot of a new reign.

The Queen wore lilac, riding with the Duke of Edinburgh and the Duke of Beaufort in the glistening first carriage of the time-honoured ritual procession. Princess Margaret and the Princess Royal rode in the second carriage. Scarlet-clad outriders, the wonderful greys, the rising cheers… People waved their programmes, aware that the first race was suitably to see Choir Boy as favourite in the Queen Anne Stakes. What a superb racing sensation to savour — Choir Boy's win for the Queen on such a day! (That morning the Mayor and Corporation and Dean and Canons of Windsor, in full panoply, had tendered congratulatory addresses to the Queen on her Accession.)

Fully demonstrating her interest in her horse, the Queen went at once to the paddock, and thus instantly staged a sharp break with tradition. The Royal Party had always unfailingly gone to the Royal Box immediately on arrival. The expectant top-hatted groups on the lawns were already respectfully turned to its windows and a laugh arose when it was realized that they had their backs to the Queen as she walked through the throng with the Duke of Edinburgh and the Duke of Norfolk. Her Majesty herself was not unamused.

She, too, was hopeful that her colt could give her first Ascot a deft auspicious opening, repeating his starry performance as the first winner of her reign. It would be a happy compliment to Captain Moore, who had bred and raced Choir Boy's dam, Choral, in Ireland. Alas, when the race was well and truly over — brilliantly won by Gordon on Southborne — Choir Boy came ignominiously labouring past the stands in the last four. The forlorn hush that met him was broken by a cascade of laughter from the Royal Box. The Queen laughed merrily at her own defeat and discomfiture and then turned to commiserate with Captain Moore.

Choir Boy alone had failed to realize what was expected of him. A few days later, he encountered the misfortune of a split pastern and he was not raced again in his third year. The following season, he ran unplaced in both the Rosebery Stakes at Kempton Park and the Victoria Cup at Hurst Park. But he brilliantly redeemed his reputation in the pages of racing history by winning the Royal Hunt Cup in Coronation year. On sentimental grounds it was considered that he might be retained at Sandringham, but late in 1953 he was sold to Señor Quarnett of Uruguay for stud. Unlike Queen Victoria, who filled her paddocks with contented pensioners, after they had been in her service a certain time, Elizabeth II showed that she intended to maintain her racing activities on a sound business footing from the start.

Throughout the rest of the accession Ascot meeting, the Queen inflicted a further defeat on the more futile outposts of hoary precedent by remaining on the course for every race. On the second day her private interest focused chiefly on a duel between her Stream of Light and the Princess Royal's Mallet in the Ribblesdale Stakes. Her aunt's horse was defeated and Stream of Light achieved third place, behind M. Boussac's Esquilla. The next day the Queen saw Aquino II win the Gold Cup, a tribute of a French horse trained in a British stable. On the Friday it seemed a far cry from Queen Victoria's entreaties to her son when the Queen walked to the paddock with the Princess Royal and the Duchess of Gloucester but remained outside the ring, casually leaning on the rails, to watch the horses parade. Many nearby racegoers were unconscious of her presence and the crowd had formed a long lane for her elsewhere. The racecourse is one of the few places where, much to her enjoyment, the Queen is not under the constant strain of being the prime focus of attention. On this occasion, an eavesdropper who overheard her comments on the horses for the Wokingham Stakes and moved away hastily, obviously hurrying to the tote, must also have made the salutary discovery that she is not omniscient. The Queen liked the look of the Aga Khan's Blue Star, which was not in the first three, and she strongly fancied No. 5. Donore, which did not win.

III

The Queen said wistfully that she would like a horse in the St. Leger but it had to be admitted there was nothing suitable in sight. And then suddenly the proposal mushroomed that Mrs. Rank might sell Gay Time to the National Stud and the colt could in turn be leased to Her Majesty. Negotiations were at their height in mid-July when the Queen went to Ascot Heath to see the remarkable return match of Tulyar and Gay Time in the King George VI and Queen Elizabeth Stakes.

Gay Time had not been seen since he was defeated so narrowly in the Derby but Tulyar had meanwhile cleaned up

120

the Eclipse Stakes. Once again the Queen watched a race of extreme excitement. One flighty entrant kicked up so much at the gate that the starter rightly decided he could wait no longer and the miscreant was left behind. At the final bend Gordon Richards was leading on Le Sage, with Gay Time just behind, and Tulyar lying third. With a quarter-mile to go the race was clearly still between the three, and the two rivals were closing on the veteran Le Sage.

At this point Piggott put Gay Time to win, passed Le Sage but still could not shake off Tulyar. Now Smirke, on Tulyar, was no longer content to bide his time and Tulyar streaked half a length before Gay Time. The latter courageously kept on gaining from yard to yard in the last hundred yards. It was finally Tulyar from Gay Time by a neck and thus the Aga Khan's great horse won in one season more stake money (£59,351) than any horse had ever won before in Britain. After that few people were in doubt that the Queen would see Gay Time at Goodwood. Incidentally, she had another moment of excitement that afternoon, staying for all the races, when in the last race Gordon on the Aga Khan's Dader and Eph Smith on Persian Wheel were both thrown. The Queen delayed leaving the course until she received reassurances of their safety.

It was twenty-three years since the reigning monarch had gone to Goodwood, and the apartments which King George V often occupied had become service and club rooms for estate workers. The former royal bathroom was a bar. Instead the Queen stayed at Arundel where the Sovereign had not been a guest, so it was said, for a century. But it is noteworthy that Her Majesty missed the opening day of the meeting so that she might call on Queen Mary at Marlborough House before the old lady left for Sandringham. Not every young woman would so willingly sacrifice a day's keen enjoyment in order to visit her grandmother.

One can count it strange that Goodwood, so admirably blending on one of the world's most beautiful racecourses the patrician and plebeian elements of the Sport of Kings, should have fallen into royal neglect. Watching over the heads of the Sussex crowd from the Duke of Richmond and Gordon's private box, listening to the commentary when the horses were out of sight, the Queen delighted in every minute. Moreover, the £50,000 purchase of Gay Time by the National Stud had been signed and sealed, together with the Queen's lease, and his royal appearance in the Gordon Stakes promised an exciting climax to the week.

In the mile or one and a half mile events on the sweeping course the starting post is practically beyond public view and the Queen took advantage of this, the second day, to motor down and watch the gate sprung at close quarters. As it moved down the course, her car was cheered to the echo. Tranquil evenings at Cowdray, watching the Duke of Edinburgh playing polo, sunny visits to Lord Rupert Nevill's seaside bungalow at Felpham, the Duke of Norfolk's Arundel Ball filled out the week with summer pleasure. Watching Gay Time saddled for the Gordon Stakes, the Queen noted the opposition, one of the Aga Khan's Nearco colts and a colt by Blue Train. But Gordon Richards ventured the opinion that there was little to beat, and he was right. Although the ace jockey had to urge his steed, the race developed into a duel with the Duchess of Norfolk's Tarr Steps, who was duly beaten by half a length, a conclusion satisfactory both to guest and hostess.

The Queen now set her heart on winning the St. Leger, a race that had proved royally elusive since her father's win with Sun Chariot in 1942. Gay Time departed for Beckhampton in clouds of disinfectant, for there had been coughing at his former stables, and moreover there was the possibility Tulyar had taken it out of him. Another Beckhampton horse, Infernal Machine — wittily named by George VI as the offspring of Dante–Golden Coach — meanwhile won a couple of races, a propitious accomplishment since this filly's dam was full sister to Sun Chariot. A second Beckhampton hopeful, Black Bee, also won the Fillies' Plate at Bath.

On the eve of the St. Leger the Queen travelled down from Balmoral in the royal train and drove to the course from Bawtry. There was the promising fact that Gordon Richards had already won five St. Legers but had not won the race for some years. As she stood with Lord Allendale in the paddock, the Queen may well have agreed with others that Tulyar and Gay Time took the honours. No other horse mattered, and Tulyar's majestic stride eclipsed everything in the canter down. When they were off, Gay Time began briskly.

With three furlongs to go, Gay Time, M. Boussac's Alcinus, and Lord Rosebery's Bob Major were racing abreast. Smirke on Tulyar was nearly boxed in behind. Then suddenly he drew out, abruptly Gay Time had nothing left and it was Tulyar's win, with Gay Time falling to fifth. The Queen lowered her glasses and laughed, but her jockey could see afterwards that deep disappointment warred with her sporting smile.

Choir Boy and Gay Time … both were disappointments despite elements of success. Gay Time was next prepared for the Champion Stakes but he worked so badly that he could not be run. As soon as he found himself leading, he faltered. It was like driving a car at high speed, Gordon Richards found, and suddenly running out of gas. Nevertheless it could be argued that he had suffered from being in four different stables and the Queen resolved to keep him in training.

Yet Her Majesty was to have one further win that season bringing her total to ten, with an aggregate of prize-money of £5,525. It came most fortuitously on the day of her first State Opening of Parliament, that occasion when a photographer snapped the Queen in her coach and so admirably caught her aglow with happiness. Within three hours there came the news that her filly High Service had won the Queen Bess Plate. What names more apt for horse or race?

That autumn, too, Noel Murless moved to Warren Place, Newmarket, making it more convenient for the Queen to watch the gallops from time to time. Motoring from Sandringham late in November, she watched the Boyd-Rochfort string, Choir Boy, Stream of Light, Aureole and the new yearlings, Festival Light, Martial Music, and Angel Bright. It was resolved, as the company reports say, to forgo Double Entry, who had faltered last in two races at Newmarket and Yarmouth. Then there were decisions to be taken on Mr. Murless's youngest stock, Landau, Rejoicing, and The Chase, and to be weighed again were the puzzling pros and cons of Gay Time.

Soon, in 1953, his early win in the March Stakes at Newmarket, ahead of the moderate Lucius and Zucchero, suggested a successful season. Yet he finished only third in the Burwell Stakes and second place was the best Gordon Richards could do with him in a Birmingham ride. Plans for the Coronation Cup, however, still went forward.

'Do you want to ride him?' Captain Moore asked Gordon.

'Not particularly,' said Gordon. 'I've had enough!'

So Breasley rode Gay Time in the Coronation Cup of Coronation year, but the horse finished fifth as if stubbornly determined to show he was through with racing. The dénouement came at Royal Ascot when he finished the third of four in the Hardwicke Stakes, with a telltale eight and ten lengths between the leaders. Later he was sold to the Japanese Government for £15,000 and shipped with a troupe of twenty-nine brood mares. It was too late to be wise after the event and say that he should have gone straight to stud when first acquired. He had proved a thoroughly bad bargain.

10: AUREOLE

I

In the cavalcade of racing honours it will surely always seem the happiest alliance of events that the Queen should have had a horse as handsome and outstanding as the majestic chestnut colt Aureole to carry her colours in Coronation year. His very name had the golden ring of intrepid Elizabethan challenge, yet it was arrived at by a brilliant inspiration at a time when the Coronation of Elizabeth II was still an undreamed-off prospect of remote future years.

One April day in 1950, when the foal was only a few days old, the then Princess Elizabeth visited the royal paddocks, befriended the little creature and cast her eye down a pedigree chart of his antecedents and kindred. Aureole was by Hyperion out of Angelola by Donatello II. The sire had cast lustre into the names as well as the performance of his progeny for a generation. The Queen considered the fresher nuances in the name of Donatello II. It was not in flattery that the President of the Royal Academy once praised the Queen's knowledge of art as 'amazing … unequalled since George III'. Though less publicized the Queen is as characteristically thorough in her love of art as in her love of racing and, casting her mind to Renaissance sculpture, seeking suggestions of radiance that would match Hyperion, she unerringly selected the apt token of Donatello's marble saints, the golden disc around their heads symbolizing glory, the aureole…

King George VI probably marvelled at his daughter's precision as he approved the name. From the first the then Princess liked the look and temperament of the shy, nervous foal. He reminded her of the old adage that had been misapplied to Hyperion:

> Three white feet, give him to your man.
> Four white feet, sell him if you can!

Aureole had three white socks as true inheritance from his sire as well as the broad white blaze that was to give him an aristocratic and even supercilious air on the racecourse. In childhood the Queen had heard Hyperion jovially talked of as 'Grandpapa's Derby winner'. This was because King George V had a Marlborough Club sweepstake ticket on him when he won the Derby in 1933 and was delighted when he drew the £100 prize. Through Hyperion and Gainsborough, Aureole stemmed from two generations of Derby winners. Could he achieve a classic hat-trick of breeding? Appraising his points, the Princess once asked in puzzlement, 'But what are his imperfections?' The colt was lightly framed, she agreed, but might fill out. Enthusiastically, as time went on, she talked of his yearling prowess to her father, unaware that the colt was destined to link two reigns.

He was not difficult to break, though he had the highly strung excitable temperament of the true champion, but the legend burgeoned among the stable-lads at Freemason Lodge that the royal newcomer was fractious and unpredictable, a bundle of nerves and a packet of problems, a tiger, a devil who would savage a boy 'if he could'. The thumb-biting savagery of Diamond Jubilee was nothing to some of the dark hints that circulated in Newmarket. On one occasion, visiting Freemason Lodge, the Queen offered her favourite an apple to crunch. A moment later, the colt bucked and kicked, amid shouts of 'Look out, your Majesty!' while members of the party scrambled to screen the Queen. This story of *lèse-majesté* has enjoyed wide circulation. The simple truth is that Aureole corresponded to Shakespeare's noble animal, 'Thin mane, thick tail, broad buttock, tender hide.' His hide was so tender, indeed, that flies were his torment. An unwary pat could set him rearing.

Keenly anxious not to disappoint his patron, Captain Boyd-Rochfort did not hurry this starlet but treated him indeed with infinite patience. It was all the more ironic that when the colt was sent at the Queen's wish to the York Ebor meeting, he was variously denounced as too green, unfit, and wild. Aureole's prima-donna temperament in the parade-ring indicated to these Jeremiahs that he had had no sort of preparation, and the impression spread that he had been entered in the Acomb Stakes at York only to accustom him to the noise and jostle of the race. Perhaps the punters caught the glint of white in his nearside eye and noticed him defying Carr towards that gate. At that moment, Aureole was available at odds of 100–8 for the only time in his career and for the only time he ran unfancied. In the race itself, a trial of six furlongs for maidens, he did nothing wrong. He was off faultlessly, drew up with the leaders at two furlongs and held all the way. A challenger named Brolly drew near in the last furlong, but Carr, with exemplary tact, refrained from using his whip and Aureole took the day. The stupefaction that greeted him was comparable only with the Queen's win of the Doncaster Cup with her 25–1 outsider Agreement several years later.

The Queen, however, was jubilant when the news was telephoned to Balmoral. The £1,500 stake money had lifted her protégé out of the red and decisively underlined his Derby entry. It is sometimes said erroneously that Aureole was never defeated as a two-year-old. The error mercifully covers the fiasco of the Middle Park Stakes when, tackling much tougher opposition, Aureole curvetted so disgracefully at the gate that he lost a couple of lengths as the tapes went up and finished only sixth, six lengths behind the winner, Royal Challenger, who fully lived up to his name with Gordon Richards.

II

Through the winter of 1952–3 the Queen must have read her trainer's reports with mingled feelings, for Aureole was to be her only home-bred three-year-old for Coronation year. The only other prospect, Double Entry, by Borealis, had fallen out after straggling last in two races at Yarmouth and Newmarket. The coming two-year-olds included Angel Bright, a full sister to Aureole, besides Festival Light, Opera Score, Rosy Glow, Beginner's Luck, and Martial Music. The yearlings seemed an exceptional crop and Captain Moore selected at least eight to go forward. In addition, the Queen leased three National Stud yearlings who would be coming out in the Coronation summer, Ariana (promptly renamed The Chase), Landau, and Rejoicing. Yet these were 'futures' and Aureole was still left the lone royal contender of the classics.

To acquaint herself closer with his idiosyncrasies the Queen twice visited Freemason Lodge that winter. He seemed to recognize his owner and accepted a sweet apple, his favourite titbit, with dignity, though not before the Queen had caught her trainer's assenting eye. No client was ever more considerate or more sympathetic with a trainer's problems. Aureole, though so highly strung, ate voraciously, and his fare had to be watched. Then there was his strange dislike for the Limekilns gallop, where he would refuse to start or, if got going, would dart sideways off the gallop unexpectedly. A few minutes on the Limekilns could unsettle him for hours. At the same time, the coppery chestnut coat was the picture of health.

129

Imperturbably Captain Boyd-Rochfort would sum up progress, undeterred by small setbacks.

Her Majesty's first racing excursion of the year was when she accompanied her husband in February to the Royal Artillery Saddle Club meeting at Larkhill, incidentally her first experience of point-to-point. With the zest of the first meeting of the season it attracted as usual some of the finest cross-country riders and the Queen thoroughly enjoyed herself, spending most of the afternoon watching beside one of the jumps. Then, in March, the Queen travelled to Cheltenham for the Gold Cup.

The saloon coach of the royal train was attached to the racegoers' excursion train, enabling the Queen to work at her papers before snatching an afternoon's pleasure. At Cheltenham she met the Queen Mother, who had been staying at Spye Park with Lady Avice Spicer, and the two royal ladies lunched with the stewards. It was Knock Hard's year and once again the Queen enjoyed the chasing in every detail, visiting the start for one race, taking a close view of the fences for another, absorbed and delightfully happy through the cold, misty afternoon.

It was on this occasion that Mr. Cazalet first presented Dick Francis to the Queen and the Queen Mother. Having firmly tied his cap on, Dick could not doff it in respect, an awkwardness he remembered long after he was winning his royal races. At Sandown Park a week later the Queen and the Queen Mother also saw Fred Winter achieve his hundredth win of the National Hunt season and sent for him to congratulate him on 'the great achievement' of a century reached so soon. But Winter was happily able to drag his headgear free in time.

These were enjoyable occasions fitted into the growing pressure of preparations for the year's great ceremony. Meanwhile the odds on Aureole shortened almost in ratio to the national mood of rejoicing. When the Queen went to Newmarket for the 2,000 Guineas, she first paid a short private visit to Freemason Lodge to find her colt in good fettle for his first classic. Accompanied by only a lady-in-waiting, the Queen had not expected the cheering crowd that filled the streets, estimated at a quarter of a million people, as if every man, woman, and child in Suffolk had turned out to greet her.

All Newmarket was acutely conscious that it was the first time in 250 years that the reigning Queen had come to watch the racing. The crowds pressed as close as possible to the Royal Box and waited while she lunched with the stewards — the Duke of Norfolk, Sir Humphrey de Trafford, and Major-General Feilden — spasmodically singing and cheering. They clapped as Her Majesty walked through a drizzle of rain to the paddock. As with Gay Time on a similar occasion, only Aureole did not seem to know what was expected. He was so skittishly restless before the start that he ran unplaced, falling behind Nearula, Bebe Grande, and Oleandrin. As Nearula passed the post, in fact, Aureole was ten lengths behind. At the same time connoisseurs noted that towards the end others were flagging. Only Nearula and Aureole were really galloping. The royal colt, they opined, would be difficult to beat over a mile and a half.

Time duly proved that Nearula, the 2–1 favourite of the Guineas, was nowhere in the Derby. Oddly enough, Pinza did not appear at Newmarket. Nor was he in the Derby Trial at Lingfield, when Aureole in calm, responsive mood pulled the field throughout the distance, raced past Mountain King (a

Derby also-ran) in the straight, and staged a superb win of no fewer than five lengths.

'That's what he needed,' said Captain Boyd-Rochfort, now becoming really hopeful of saddling his first Derby winner. Aureole had achieved a significant success and a significant failure. 'It's all terribly exciting, isn't it?' said the Queen, shaking hands with the newly knighted Sir Gordon Richards in the Epsom paddock.

The Coronation Derby was held only four days after the Coronation itself. The Queen's colt Rejoicing which had been expected to win the Holiday Stakes at Kempton Park on Coronation Day had not quite pulled it off. The Queen's last racing excursion when still uncrowned had been a visit with her mother to Hurst Park — sandwiched between Abbey rehearsals — to see Galloway Braes win the Queen Elizabeth Steeplechase on May 25th. 'You had them all strung out like a lot of carthorses!' she told Robert Morrow, the jockey, afterwards. Hopefully the Mayor and Corporation of Epsom had suggested that the Queen should drive down to the Derby by road to be royally received in Epsom town, but the police frowned at the possible disruption of Derby Day traffic and the Queen arrived by train.

It was just as well. Freed at last from the heavy strain of ceremonial, the Queen relaxed for the first time after a series of exhausting fifteen-hour days that had been crammed with audiences, investitures, drives, and appearances. Unlike the downpour of Coronation Day, the Epsom Downs basked in royal weather. As she stepped into the Royal Box, a bower decked in banners of blue and gold massed about by hydrangeas, the Queen and her husband were gravely presented with special racecards bound in red leather with the royal cipher embossed in gold. The Duke of Edinburgh pretended to be surprised at learning of twenty-seven runners.

'You'd think there were only two horses in the race,' he said. 'No one talks of any of the others.'

In actual fact, Sir Victor Sassoon's Pinza and Brigadier Wyatt's Premonition were joint favourites, with Aureole second favourite. But Nearula, Good Brandy, and Novarullah all had their followers. But the Queen, with extraordinary insight, commented to Norman Bertie, Pinza's trainer, 'Aureole hasn't only Pinza to watch. There's also the French colt, Pink Horse.'

Pink Horse was rated a 33–1 outsider. Yet Pinza won by four lengths with Aureole second and, a length and a half behind, Pink Horse was third. If the Queen had inherited Bowes-Lyon prevision, her guess could not have been closer.

Sir Gordon looked numb as he was led in, as if dazed by the overwhelming reception. Pinza was the only horse, a wit said, to carry a knight and beat a Queen. The four-length win was clearly not a fluke. On the other hand, if Aureole's defeat had been the subject of an inquest, the verdict might well have been that Coronation fervour cost the Queen the race.

For Aureole paraded calmly but as he left the paddock an ebullient racegoer dealt him a good luck pat — which Carr afterwards described as more like a hearty clout — that in all probability decided the day. Aureole reacted so violently that it took Harry Carr and two stable-lads all their work to steady him. And after that it was Pinza's race.

Early on, a good position seemed to elude the colt as though he were scarcely trying. Carr brought him to ninth at the top of the hill and urged him into the first six at Tattenham Corner. The Queen jumped up and down in her excitement, her black-gloved hand tight on the rail. Then Aureole went steadily on but the run was too late. However, the Queen had won £2,000 and was instantly delighted that her horse should be beaten in the good cause of giving Gordon the first Derby win of all his twenty-eight attempts. Her Majesty's unfeigned pleasure in congratulating him showed no trace of disappointment.

'And I suppose you're going to retire now that you've won the Derby?' the Duke of Edinburgh put in.

'Of course not!' said the Queen. 'He's going to ride Landau for me in the Derby next year.'

III

Only ten days divided the Coronation Derby and the 1953 Royal Ascot, ten days packed for the Queen with every conceivable royal duty, from a service of thanksgiving in St. Paul's to a Review of the Fleet. Yet she enjoyed each of the four days of Royal Ascot with irresistible zest — and then arrived quietly, unofficially, almost unnoticed, to watch the Saturday racing, staying till after the last race.

The Ascot house-party at Windsor, too, had a special quality of happiness and beauty that year with the inclusion of several of the Coronation maids-of-honour among the Queen's younger friends. Though torrential rain flooded the greensward, causing the second day's royal procession to be cancelled, the Queen, quite undeterred, steadfastly made her way to the parade-ring and unsaddling enclosure, missing nothing. It was the year when Choir Boy atoned for his earlier failings by winning the Royal Hunt Cup, beating Sir Gordon Richards' mount, Brunetto. Next day Sir Gordon received not a few wildly preposterous letters from people thanking him for being nice and letting the Queen win after beating Aureole.

Telling the Queen of this absurdity on the Friday, before he saddled her hopeful Landau for the Windsor Castle Stakes, Sir

Gordon found Her Majesty much amused. Happily there was nothing to disturb the Jockey Club in Landau's failure in the Windsor Castle, nor in Gay Time's funeral march to third place in the Hardwicke Stakes, that same afternoon.

Next, after her Coronation tours of Scotland, Northern Ireland, and Wales, the Queen went to Sandown Park with the Princess Royal to see Aureole in the Eclipse Stakes. She was by no means sure of him. He had been coughing slightly and lagging at gallops but the Eclipse is a valuable race that often turns Derby defeats into wins. Besides, the Queen wished to decide for herself whether he was ripe for another bout with Pinza and, for once, the result still left her in doubt.

Aureole only just managed to stride into third place, ten lengths behind the winner. The Queen awaited reports from her trainer, and it was only on the day before the King George VI and Queen Elizabeth Stakes that she decided to let Aureole run.

His near eclipse in the Eclipse had wound him up. At Ascot with the Queen Mother and Princess Margaret, the Queen talked confidently to Carr. But Derby history repeated itself.

This time, not a racegoer's pat but a hefty kick in the ribs from the French horse, Pharel, led to trouble. Aureole reared in a panic, with such sudden violence just as Carr was mounting that the jockey went flying. Fortunately the Queen had just left the paddock and did not see this indignity. Rubbing himself ruefully, awaiting the vet's all clear, he was unavoidably late at the start. A race worth £23,000 means £2,300 to the winning jockey and Carr must have seen this windfall dissolving before his eyes. Once they were away, Aureole did nothing amiss. Yet again Pinza won by nearly four lengths, repeating Derby form to the ounce.

Was there ever a colt more exciting and more exasperating, so strong in potential, so remiss in achievement? At Goodwood House, where the Queen stayed with the Duke and Duchess of Richmond and Gordon throughout racing week, Her Majesty discussed her problem with her host and hostess. The rooms over the Adam library of the old Sussex house had been dexterously rearranged as a three-room royal guest suite, and in the Queen's retiring room the Duchess happened to have arranged a little gallery of horse pictures remindful of other ambiguous colts who had proved classic winners.

The week developed into a pleasant pattern of racegoing followed by visits to Cowdray to watch Prince Philip playing polo. On the second day both the Queen and Prince Philip saw Choir Boy run unplaced in the Drayton Handicap as if adding an extra line to a chapter. Before the races on the final day the Queen held a Privy Council at Goodwood House. It was 328 years since Charles I held a Council at Wilton and since then, it seemed, a Council had only twice been held in a private house. On the first occasion, Edward VII held a Council at Lord Londonderry's home, the sole business being to declare Lord Londonderry Lord President of the Council. On the second occasion, King George V held a Council at Goodwood to settle an Irish boundary adjustment. Now, twenty-nine years later to the day, the Gobelins tapestries in the drawing-room gazed down on his granddaughter. Under Edward VII, Sir Almeric FitzRoy complained sadly of having to travel 500 miles in twenty-four hours to assist in a ceremony occupying ten seconds. But the Queen was concerned with the end-of-season accumulation of Parliamentary business and no hardship was entailed for Lord Salisbury or Lord de la Warr, travelling from his Sussex home. If the Queen intended a compliment to her hostess, she could scarcely have bettered the occasion.

The Queen, Prince Philip and the Privy Councillors afterwards lunched in the Duke of Richmond's pavilion overlooking the racecourse. Lord Salisbury subsequently returned to London, but Mr. W. G. Agnew, the newly appointed Clerk of the Privy Council, was free to enjoy an afternoon's racing with his father-in-law, Captain Moore.

At the same time, Captain Moore was concerned with the return of Gay Time to the National Stud and thus Goodwood provided a key to the Aureole riddle. Gay Time had been under treatment at the patient hands of a Harley Street consultant, Mr. Charles Brook, and the question of his further professional services arose. Although unavoidably curtailed in Gay Time's case, the therapy showed results. Why not a course of treatment for Aureole? The Queen agreed and thus set in gear a future placing and five wins in six events.

IV

Mr. Charles Brook's methods were unconventional but they stood upon results. His theories of nervous tension, invisible yet real as in the mainspring of a watch and equally amenable to adjustment or 'impulse change', had been effectively demonstrated with an awkward squad of Coronation procession horses. Cavalry horses and hacks, they were destined to carry V.I.P. riders, some of whom had not climbed astride a saddle for years. One old horse had been lame for weeks without dismaying his young accustomed rider, who adapted himself to the up-and-down movement. With visions of a veteran general flying over Tarracona's head, Mr. Brook had restored him to normality in fourteen days. Then there was Blaze, who shivered with nerves at the martial music and crowd noises of the test parades, and Easy Race, a confirmed puller. The first improved in confidence, the second ceased to pull from the first treatment. Add to this a horse named Endless Rush who, from a too acute fear of flag waving progressed to becoming too self-assertive and one had confirmation of the claim that adverse nervous impulses could be replaced by a beneficial new tide through the practitioner's hands.

But could he transform Aureole? Could he cure the colt's habit of wildly wolfing his food or diminish the prospect that a stable-boy might be sent flying, as once before, with a powerful flick of the nuzzle? Six times a week, that August, the calm bearded therapist stood in Aureole's stall, his fingers on withers, neck, or stomach. Soon Captain Boyd-Rochfort's reports to Balmoral spoke encouragingly of progress. The horse was eating better, and putting on weight. Hopes were improving for the St. Leger.

For weeks beforehand, in fact, it was anticipated that Doncaster would see another great duel between Aureole and Pinza. At the gallops Aureole always finished brightly ahead of his stable companion, Brigadier Wyatt's Premonition. As all the world knows, Pinza broke down and was scratched in St. Leger week and Aureole's odds toughened drastically.

For the second time, the Queen came down from Balmoral, cheered tempestuously along the Yorkshire roads. Lunching with Lord and Lady Scarborough at Sandbeck Park, Her Majesty met Sir Winston and Lady Churchill, who were celebrating their forty-fifth wedding anniversary. Again a Privy Council was held. (Goodwood *and* Doncaster, moped a dour minority, unaware of a journey to Scotland considerately avoided for Mr. Agnew.) No Prime Minister had visited Town Moor since Disraeli and the Corporation had embellished their banked red, white, and blue coronation flowers with a welcoming floral V for victory. There were presentations of Doncaster butterscotch to take home to Prince Charles and Princess Anne and, smiling happily, the Queen learned that Aureole showed no strain from his journey.

Then the second race was won by her Murless colt Landau, a two-year-old who seemed to win irresistibly whenever the effort was asked. Was it a good omen — or a compensation?

The Queen watched Aureole saddled, and when she returned to the Royal Box uncommonly sharp eyes claimed that Premonition and Northern Light II were marked on her programme as the favourite's chief rivals.

A spatter of rain fell and a racegoer suddenly opened an umbrella right under Aureole's nose. Remarkably, the horse did not flinch though a few months earlier the incident would have wrought havoc. But what was worse Carr kept him on a no-nonsense rein and the colt imperiously decided to resent this mastery, so much so that he veered from the parade and went frantically down the course.

The Queen whistled softly as he cantered past the Royal Box, fighting for his head. Firmly, Carr succeeded in exercising restraint and got him to the start without mishap. In that moment the Queen perhaps already swallowed disappointment. After the 'off', she watched Aureole still pulling, refusing to settle down. Her glasses went tighter to her eyes as he moved up from seventh to third place, but his baulked determination had drained his powers too soon. Carr did well to get him in, behind Northern Light II and the Freemason Lodge winner, Premonition. And Captain Boyd-Rochfort's irreproachable manner was never better displayed than when he commiserated with his Queen on her defeat and accepted her congratulations — bestowed with a broad smile — on winning for another client.

All the same, the Captain desperately wanted Aureole to win something sound for the Queen in what remained of Coronation year. Judiciously he entered the capricious colt in the weight-for-age Cumberland Stakes at the Ascot October meeting. Carr could not make the weight and Eph Smith was substituted. The rest is simply told. Aureole seemed more intent on waltzing than on racing at the start but he got away. Skyraider held the lead until two furlongs from home, with ten furlongs safely covered, and then Aureole effortlessly went to the front and stayed there.

It was an unequivocal victory that abruptly opened a broad new panorama of prospective four-year-old honours. Meanwhile preparations for the round-the-world Commonwealth tour were intensifying, and it was not until twelve days before the date of take-off from London Airport that Her Majesty could slip away and visit Noel Murless with Captain Moore. The training for five newly leased National Stud yearlings had to be mapped and then there was Landau, that white hope of the 2,000 Guineas and the Derby. To cover all eventualities, Rejoicing was agreed as second choice, although at times Owen Tudor's grey-coated son reminded the Queen irresistibly of a camel.

After lunch the Queen went on to Sandringham, where new stables were being built, but a day or two later she was back in Newmarket, pondering the three-year-old prospects of Festival Light and Angel Bright, both of whom were engaged for the 1,000 Guineas and the Oaks. Among the yearlings soon graduating to the Boyd-Rochfort two-year-old string, the Queen best liked the look of Alexander, Sierra Nevada, and Biscuit. The royally named Ermine, on the other hand, seemed unaware of her status as the daughter of Kingstone and Astrakhan. With this one doubt, the Queen could nevertheless look forward with great expectations. In Coronation year, her horses had won five races and she had won £4,913 as an owner and £4,100 as a breeder.

Moreover, only the weekend before she left with Prince Philip for Newfoundland and Bermuda, the Queen had another enjoyable day with the Queen Mother and Princess Margaret at Sandown Park. Racegoers cheered her happily and called '*Bon voyage!*' With the Queen Mother's M'as-Tu-Vu in winning form, the Royal Party watched from one of the hurdles and remained after the racing to see the schooling over the fences. Every fresh facet of thoroughbred training and performance absorbed the Queen. And with the racing attainments of the year so satisfyingly behind her, it could all indeed be voted 'a lot of fun'.

11: LANDAU

I

The intense strain of the 1953-4 Commonwealth tour was happily leavened by at least four race-meetings at which the Queen presented the gold trophy of the main event, and those close to Her Majesty discovered that her reputation of racing knowledge was no legend. Discussing privileged Australian guests who should share the Royal Box at Flemington, an official frantically telephoned: 'For Pete's sake, put in someone who really knows the form and the stud book. Her Majesty has it all pat.' At Randwick, just before the start of the Queen Elizabeth Stakes, the Queen was attracted by the look of an outsider named Blue Ocean. 'He walks like a champion,' she observed. The colt was from an obscure mare and had done most of his racing on the smaller country tracks. That afternoon he nevertheless justified royal recognition by breaking the course record by one and a quarter seconds and equalling the Australian record of two minutes twenty-seven and three-quarter seconds for one and a half miles.

At Flemington, too, the Queen duly saw a mile five furlongs won by a horse named Cromie, aided adeptly by a stable companion. 'That's as pretty a piece of team-work as one could wish to see,' she observed, and animatedly discussed the advantages of a pacemaker over the distance. Earlier, at Trentham, in New Zealand, people had stood ten deep in front of the stands to watch the Queen while she watched the races and at Ellerslie one race was suitably won by Royal Applause.

Her Majesty's New Zealand hosts quickly found that the Queen could expertly tell who got away badly, who got the run of a race, and who got pocketed. By royal request, a trotting race was staged at Addington, a track the Queen had often heard her father praise, and the Duke of Edinburgh started a race named in his honour. Smilingly the Queen confessed that she had practically worn out her collection of New Zealand training films by running the reels over and over. In her library was the film *A New Zealand Thoroughbred*, and the Queen was on familiar ground when she visited its location, the Alton Lodge stud of Sir James Fletcher, where she patted the champion New Zealand stallion, Balloch, and inspected the twenty-year-old English Derby winner, Midday Sun. At the Ta Rapa stud of the Malcolm brothers, similarly, the Queen saw the Precipitation horse, Summertime, whose dam Great Truth had been bred at Hampton Court. Truly Her Majesty was not so far from home.

Throughout the tour, indeed, messages from Hampton unfailingly kept her in touch with her still closer racing interests. Landau sometimes resisted 'driving' but progress was promising. Aureole was still eating well. In New Zealand the Queen heard that Choir Boy had safely embarked for Uruguay. At Fremantle came the not unexpected news that Ermine had failed to justify his place of honour as the Queen's first runner of the season, and had provided a miserable showing as a turgid also-ran in the Maiden Fillies Plate. Amid the rough waters of the Cocos-Keeling Islands, the Queen heard that Landau had been only third in a field of five in the Column Produce Stakes. A rainy March had held up his gallops, but there seemed no excuse for him when he lost the 2,000 Guineas three weeks later.

Not until the Queen reached Uganda at the end of April, in fact, did her first winner appear. Then the homely news was radioed that Corporal, a handsome two-year-old chestnut bred at Hampton from Court Martial–Carmen, had won the May Maidens Stakes the first day at Newmarket, scotching a heavy field and in particular defeating Light Harvest by a length. Two days later, the Queen was again successful when the three-year-old Opera Score, another of Carmen's offspring, won the Somersham Stakes in an exciting neck-and-neck finish with Shubra, a notable riding feat for Masters, a young Boyd-Rochfort apprentice.

These events heightened the Queen's natural anxiety to get home. The package of action photographs of the Somersham had scarcely reached Malta than Aureole headed the Victor Wild Stakes by four lengths, and that same afternoon the Hampton two-year-old Biscuit won the Minting Stakes at Kempton Park. This pleasurable double not only demonstrated Aureole's rapidly reforming character but subtly enhanced the happiness of the Queen's reunion voyage with her children.

Meanwhile, Australian Turf writers were still eagerly assessing the Queen's 'knowledgeable observations on type, conformation, and pedigree', her 'high degree of selective judgment', her 'almost fanatical interest in the thoroughbred'. It all gave colour to the story that as the royal yacht sailed up the English Channel, *Britannia* radioed the Admiralty, 'The Queen wishes to know how her horse got on at Lingfield this afternoon.'

The news was good, for Landau had run well in the Derby Trial Stakes, second only to Rowston Manor.

The next day a tumultuous welcome greeted the Queen and Prince Philip on their return to London, and Londoners cheered for them on the Palace balcony until well into the afternoon. Shortly afterwards messages were handed to both the Queen and her husband that caused further delight in the royal drawing-room. The Queen's mare Angel Bright, daughter of Hyperion and Angelola, had won the Oaks Trial Stakes and Prince Philip's yacht *Bluebottle* had smartly won a sailing race at Cowes.

II

With sixteen royal horses in his charge, apart from yearlings, Captain Boyd-Rochfort had so far made the running of the season and Mr. Noel Murless was to encounter some moments of acute dismay before establishing his own due proportion of wins from the eight horses in training in the Queen's National Stud string. Although the five two-year-olds, Jardiniere, Annie Oakley, Whirligig, Perambulator, and Abergeldie seemed promising, not one of them was to win a single race that year. The three-year-olds, Landau, Rejoicing, and The Chase, also caused many heads to be shaken and ultimately everything seemed to hinge on the jet-black, enigmatic Landau.

No National Stud horse had perhaps attracted such notice since the classic scoop of Big Game and Sun Chariot. The Stud had been a component of the continuity of royal racing tradition ever since Colonel Hall-Walker, its founder, leased Minoru to Edward VII from his famous Tully stud. Now it was just forty years since Hall-Walker had first offered Tully to the nation, with its complete bloodstock contents of two stallions, thirty brood mares, thirty yearlings and foals, and the additional premises of the Russley racing stables in Wiltshire. The offer was for a purchase, not a gift, and it is not to be wondered at if MPs of the day, a war on their hands, demurred at the proposition. Colonel Hall-Walker, afterwards Lord Wavertree, persisted, however, in a firm belief that the prestige of the British thoroughbred would be enhanced by the retention of his stud as the nucleus of a national institution.

145

Russley Park itself, as he saw it, could become a depot for government stallions for the cavalry.

First one and then another government department declined his offer. Shrugging his shoulders, Hall-Walker directed that all his thoroughbreds should be entered at the Newmarket December sales in 1915 and the catalogues were already distributed when the Board of Agriculture wired an acceptance of all the bloodstock and properties. The £74,000 purchase of the Tully stud caused a storm, as such figures always do, and the Stud commenced its new career under War Office aegis more the subject of criticism than congratulation.

Early in the 1930's the sensational career of the speedy Myrobella attracted a more favourable reaction. Myrobella, when leased by Lord Lonsdale, won nearly £17,000 in a year and thus, under the stock contract, some £6,000 for the Exchequer. In seventeen years, it was found, the Stud had netted 417,894 guineas from the sale of 356 yearlings and had bred the winners of 600 races accruing £300,000 in stakes. An historian might cite as an error of policy the yearling auction of the great Blandford for 730 guineas, for he was afterwards to sire four Derby winners, among them Bahram and Windsor Lad. Mistakes can, however, occur on both sides. The Aga Khan once paid £17,000 for a National Stud colt which never raced.

The Stud progeny have now won every race of merit except the Derby. Freed from Army estimates, Sir Henry Greer, the first Director, helped to accumulate a surplus of £86,000. Though this was eroded by lean years, a wit recently described the Stud under the capable management of Mr. Peter Burrell as the first nationalized industry to make a profit on its own four legs. A decisive milestone came in 1943, when the stock was transferred from Tully to lush new pastures at Gillingham,

Dorset, where much progress has been made in fertility and development research. The prime policy is admittedly not to improve profit but to improve the quality and thus the prestige of the British thoroughbred throughout the world. 'If there were no National Stud, it would be necessary to create one,' summed up a parliamentary committee in 1955.

The leasing of a choice of yearlings to the Queen is a felicitous arrangement, for the Queen pays all training fees and expenses but returns one-third of all prize money to the Stud. Thus every one of her subjects can share with the Queen a personal interest in every National Stud horse running under the royal colours.

Mr. Noel Murless trained all Her Majesty's National Stud horses ever since that astonishing year when he took over Beckhampton as a young man of thirty-eight and headed the list of winning trainers in his first season with sixty-three races won, worth £67,000. A pupil of Hubert Hartigan, of the Irish racing family, he had begun training at twenty-five in that nursery of the thoroughbred, the North Riding, and he confesses that as a Cheshire farmer's son he had never wanted to do anything else. At Beckhampton, he felt too 'southern', almost homesick. His parents were still in the North, looking after his stud, and his wife, once known in riding circles as Miss Gwen Carlow, had the Scottish hills in her blood. When Warren Place, on the crown of Newmarket Heath, came on the market, it seemed a sensible compromise. And what couple could have refused the house with its panelling and lattice windows, the stable buildings with the clocktower and deep dormer windows, the atmosphere of modernity and efficient comfort? The place had been built for Sam Darling at a cost of £92,000 and improved by the Maharajah of Baroda. It was *waiting*. Since he moved into Warren Place, the prize winnings

of the Murless-trained horses have brought over £45,000 to
the Queen.

III

In the middle of his forehead, the saturnine Landau bore white
flecks which occasionally suggested to the fanciful that the
characteristics he inherited from his parents, Dante and Sun
Chariot, by Hyperion, had stamped him with a question-mark
in reverse, a question made even more mystifying by a smudge.
He was born a seedy, peckish foal who refused to thrive,
watched with concern by the vets until they put him on a
course of aureomycin. Within six weeks he was the best-
conditioned youngster at stud, his black coat the glossiest, his
behaviour the friskiest, and the Queen early selected him as a
budding champion of high prospects. Gordon Richards found
him cocky at work but Mr. Murless brought him out early in
his first season in the Spring Stakes at Newmarket and Landau
responded by running third.

On the day that she knighted Sir Gordon, as he rose from
the accolade, the Queen said, 'I see you had a good day at
Brighton yesterday,' referring to his three winners, and then
enquired if he thought he would win on Landau on the
following Friday. Her newly knighted jockey replied doubtfully
and it seemed to the Queen that he pulled a face.

'Now why did he do that?' Her Majesty asked Captain Moore
afterwards. 'Do you think he doesn't like the horse?'

Sir Gordon had been unaware of his grimace. 'It's not as bad
as that,' he told Captain Moore. 'It must mean I wasn't very
sure.' But Landau won the £765 Fulborne Stakes in good style
from Call Girl and Gold Rain. Later, as I have told, he won the
£1,714 Doncaster Produce Stakes in some recompense to the
Queen on the day that Aureole failed to win the St. Leger.

Then he went on to pick up the Boscawen Stakes at Newmarket and altogether contributed £4,200 to Her Majesty's winnings that year.

The question-marked Landau of 1954 seemed, however, a different horse from the challenging tyro. The fiasco of his appearance in the Column Produce could not be explained by the heavy going in training or the weight he was giving away. (He had ended the previous season with equal third place in the Free Handicap at nine stone four pounds.) In the 2,000 Guineas he was joint third favourite at 8–1 with Darius, who had beaten him by a neck to third place in his Spring Stakes debut the year before. But Darius was first, ahead of Ferriol and Poona, while Landau was bunched at sixth, and Sir Gordon looked glum as he took him in. The run had been marred by an incident almost as strange as the dramatic freeze that overtook Devon Loch, for at one point Landau stopped dead in his tracks and dropped his bit. After that, there was no making up for lost ground.

'Landau! He ought to be made to pull one!' came the inevitable jeers.

Meanwhile, all the surmise of the Derby was building to the usual crescendo. Murless considered the possibility of scratching his unimpressive charge, but Rejoicing, the alternative, seemed equally below the prospects. To deprive the Queen of her interest in the Derby seemed unthinkable and wiser counsels prevailed. Whereupon Landau did so well in the Derby Trial Stakes that he was second to Rowston Manor, as I have said, the odds rebounded, and many voices were heard, full of confidence.

Some of the assurances and prognostications troubled the Queen, who does not like to feel that any racegoer may be buoyed by unwise promises on her horses. Besides, fresh difficulties had occurred backstage. Sir Gordon had been thrown heavily at Salisbury, a curious presage of the accident that was to end his riding career two months later, and he reluctantly had to decide that he would not be fit to ride Landau. The names of Rickaby and Snaith were submitted to the Queen for her decision. And it was Snaith, a boy from a council school who had started as a half a crown a week apprentice, who received the Queens' good wishes when she flew south from Balmoral to see the race that had caused such dispute and doubt.

The odds on Landau had veered from 10–1 to as long as 28–1 but he started as fourth favourite at 19–2. Following Aureole's progress, Landau had also been placed under Charles Brook's strange, passive therapy of impulse change, and he looked well in the paddock, displaying none of the caprice that had tired him on an earlier occasion.

The Queen's marked card, a subscription service of forecast selections, bore a dot for a win against Rowston Manor, with Landau second and Darius third. This was indeed precisely the position at Tattenham Corner and Landau for a brief moment had the lead in the straight.

Never have leaders been overwhelmed so swiftly. In the field was another colt who ranked Nearco among his grandparents, a 33–1 outsider named Never Say Die. Even his American owner, Mr. R. S. Clark, was flabbergasted when he heard that this unpromising Kentucky-bred colt had won. But in September his stamina was proved for all time when he won the St. Leger by ten lengths and Mr. Clark ended second only to the Queen as leading owner of the year.

Any number of theories were advanced to explain Landau's failure. A sweet tooth, it was said, had led him into a passion for jam tarts and although the stable-lads at Lingfield showed him a whole boxful of tarts to galvanize him into action, there were no jam tarts on view at Epsom. As if remembering his tastes, the Queen opened her handbag to give him a caramel. But perhaps Landau was not alone in his predilections for there were caramels similarly as a booby-prize for Angel Bright after the Oaks, when the Queen watched the rout of her Boyd-Rochfort filly far behind Mme Forget's Sun Gap.

Unfortunately the Queen was not present at Epsom's brightest royal moment of 1954 when Aureole won the Coronation Cup. Unlike Landau the previous day, Aureole not only took the lead at Tattenham Corner but romped home magnificently, five lengths ahead of his nearest rival Chatsworth. It was Aureole's first appearance since the Cumberland Stakes in October, a fine first flourish for all the garlands the Queen was convinced he would shortly wear.

The victories of Aureole and the vicissitudes of Landau were to run parallel, indeed, through that memorable summer. Between Epsom and Ascot, the days were crowded but the Queen paid a fleeting visit to Hurst Park to see the Queen Elizabeth Handicap Steeplechase with the Queen Mother. Royal Ascot itself was zestful with excitement. On the opening day Rejoicing was favourite in the Britannia Stakes, despite no better earlier success than a trivial race at York. But the Queen was not surprised when an outsider, Minstrel, won and Rejoicing ran unplaced. Her Majesty confessed to Sir Gordon that the horse reminded her of a camel, and the jockey ventured, 'Yes, ma'am, and I think he gallops like one, too.'

Walking back and forth to the paddock, the Queen enjoyed every instant and remained until after the last race. For the first time in many years the sparkle of the full carriage procession was seen on all four days. On the Wednesday Angel Bright ran unplaced in the Coronation Stakes and the third day saw the equal rout of the two-year-old Narcissus (so named from Borealis–Vanity Fair). But Friday, June 18th, brought the Queen one of the greatest racing days she had ever known.

A moderate failure was counted on when Sir Gordon Richards rode Landau over the Derby distance in the Rous Memorial Stakes, but to the Queen's delight her Murless protégé walked away from his nearest opponent with a clear four lengths. The lessee's share of the £1,340 prize at last retrieved the royal expenses on the lease. Then the gallant two-year-old Corporal, son of Court Martial and the Hampton mare Carmen, was second in the Windsor Castle Stakes.

Eager and pleased the Queen went down to the paddock to see Aureole saddled for the Hardwicke Stakes. His condition was not without concern, for the colt had undergone a minor mishap in his box a few days earlier, slightly injuring his eye.

'How do you rate our chances?' the Queen asked her jockey, Eph Smith.

'Well, ma'am,' answered Smith, who wore a hearing aid, 'we are rather handicapped. The animal is blind in one eye and I am deaf!'

The Queen laughed heartily. However, the real danger was M. Boussac's Janitor, to whom Aureole had to concede seven pounds. And when Janitor put on a spurt halfway up the straight, drew level, and then gained a slight lead, Smith ventured everything and drew his whip. Considering Aureole's temperament, it was a flick that must have made the Queen hold her breath. Aureole lunged forward afresh and the two seemed to pass the post together.

The judge, Major Petch, called for camera evidence. A tense hush fell over the stands ... and then a tumultuous cheer as the verdict for Aureole went up and M. Boussac doffed his grey topper to the Queen.

'That's the second narrow shave we've had today,' a member of the royal party told M. Boussac. The remark puzzled him until he heard that the Queen had narrowly escaped running into a low-slung telephone wire while galloping that morning on the course. Nor did this entirely end the thrills of Ascot. On the Saturday the Queen was on the heath with the Queen Mother and Princess Margaret to see the performance of Martial Music (Court Martial–Choral) in the Albemarle Stakes. Far from martial on this occasion, she straggled in last of eleven runners.

Three weeks later, when the Duke of Edinburgh was racing *Bluebottle* at Cowes, the Queen took a Saturday afternoon off at Sandown to see Sir Gordon riding Landau in the Eclipse and then the two-year-old filly Abergeldie in the Star Stakes. Landau ran with resolution in the Eclipse and, though not equal to his Ascot form, he paced King of the Tudors and Darius steadily before he came in third.

Yet this was Sir Gordon's last race as jockey. The Queen commiserated with him on not winning, watched Abergeldie saddled and returned to her box. On the gravel track towards the course and the stands the filly half-reared. 'Let her go,' said Sir Gordon to his head lad, and the horse reared again. Up and over, rolling, with the supreme jockey underneath.

Captain Moore gravely had to tell the Queen of the accident. Returning to Windsor, awaiting the X-ray, she could not leave the telephone, and sent a written message down to the hospital for the patient to receive as soon as possible. A fractured pelvis needs all the cheerfulness that can be mustered. Twice during the week the Queen sympathetically asked her racing manager to visit the hospital to convey her well wishes and encouragement. But at Ascot the following Saturday, with the accident so much in mind, it was a moment of appalling alarm for the Queen when Aureole took a leaf from Abergeldie's book and suddenly shied in the same way, depositing Eph Smith in the mud.

Luckily unhurt, the jockey scrambled up and gave chase. Galloping down the course, Aureole bumped himself on the rails and then quietly munched grass till Smith seized the reins. The old demon Aureole would have caused greater fuss. But the colt had behaved perfectly in the parade and submitted to be ridden to the gate. The occasion was the King George VI and Queen Elizabeth Stakes with its rich first prize of £23,302. Every expert eye noted his hard, supreme condition, the fine line down his quarters, the frame of ribs beneath his silky skin. He was favourite at 9–2 yet Smith had his hands full. At the start both Aureole and his stable-mate Premonition were reluctant to line up. Then the tapes rose and Aureole whipped sideways. At least eight lengths were lost and he was the last of the seventeen starters to get into his stride.

Ahead were such rivals as Chatsworth, Janitor, Darius, and Vamos. Within a mile, Aureole was lying third, almost swimming third, one might say, such was the mud after a heavy shower, and he skimmed down the straight like a meteor to win by three parts of a length from Mme Volterra's Vamos, with Darius third. 'If it hadn't been for the slush,' Smith said afterwards, 'we should have won by half a furlong.'

On duty at an international athletics meeting at the White City, Prince Philip missed sharing this unforgettable experience. 'It was wonderful,' said the Queen. 'Truly tremendously exciting. I hope all Sandringham were on it.' With Her Majesty's compliments, a case of champagne arrived at the Press Room and, since there were not enough glasses to go round, beakers and mugs were mustered to cope with it. Outside, the rain pelted down again as the racegoers cheered.

Blinded by umbrellas, racegoers narrowly missed running into the Queen as she splashed happily back from the unsaddling. Altogether Aureole had won seven races, proving himself the best horse in Europe, and securing for the Queen the major slice of the £40,993 that placed Her Majesty at the top of the 1954 owners' list.

There was a suggestion that Aureole should take part in the Washington, D.C. International at Laurel Park in which he might have proved himself the best horse in the world. But Her Majesty decided that he had done enough and this right royal horse was retired to the lush forage of a Sandringham meadow. A bronze statuette of Aureole by Herbert Haseltine stands in the Queen's private apartments and I believe he is the only racehorse so proudly honoured.

IV

Next, in this crowded summer, the Queen and her husband stayed at Arundel for the Goodwood meeting where, on the first day, the Queen narrowly watched Opera Score running to no great purpose in the Craven Handicap and a journalist narrowly watched the Queen. 'The Queen watched all six races,' he recorded. 'She frowns with concentration. She laughs with pleasure. She looks confidential as she exchanges information with trainer or jockey. She is not given to gesticulation normally but as she watches the horses her hands speak.' With less rhetoric, the Queen gave Landau a pat of pleasure when he won the £1,034 Sussex Stakes. (He had already picked up the £742 Ellesmere prize at Newmarket.) Beaming at his wife's victory, Prince Philip left Goodwood for Cowdray and polo, but, by the following day, he had left by air for his three-weeks' tour of Canada, such is the intensity of modern royal travel. That perhaps gave the Queen an idea.

Aureole was going into retirement, but why should not Landau, as a National Stud champion, carry the royal colours to America?

The Queen held a Privy Council at Arundel as she had at Goodwood House the previous year. At the auctioning, after the racing, of Intent, winner of the Findon Selling Stakes, she was an interested spectator and entered into eager discussion when the hammer fell at 1,800 guineas. Yet the Landau problem remained. Recent wins seemed to have demonstrated another of his eccentricities. When running honestly, he seemed to race better on a turning course than on the straight and the looped Laurel Park track seemed made for him.

With Aureole in mind, the Queen also accepted an invitation to visit the Sledmere Stud and spent an intensive three days as the guest of Sir Richard and Lady Sykes. Deeply interested in the Hyperion foals, she was absorbed by the patterns that had similarly appeared in Aureole and motored with relish to see another offspring of the veteran at Mr. Wickham-Boynton's stud at Burton Agnes. The Queen was not at the St. Leger and by the end of September had again lost her place as winning owner to Mr. Clark. Meanwhile, Landau was under treatment, resting his head heavily on Mr. Brook's shoulder twice a week until the therapist ached, and the Laurel Park invitation was accepted.

Then came the first October meeting, when Newmarket was without its coat of wartime camouflage paint at last. Besides Landau, the Queen had three runners: the hitherto unraced Jardiniere from Warren Place, the filly Festival Light from Freemason Lodge — neither of whom immediately rewarded Her Majesty's interest — and the sturdy Corporal, who promptly won the Foal Stakes, worth £1,102, and so restored the Queen as winning owner in the ding-dong struggle with Mr. Clark.

The entry of Landau in the Old Rowley Stakes seemed hazardous, for this was on the Rowley Mile, already the scene of Landau's three poorest races. With Snaith up, however, Landau had to face only three other runners, Marshal Ney, Narrator and Tale of Two Cities, and naturally the Queen's horse was favourite against this opposition. Alas, to his shame, Landau surrendered after a struggle at five furlongs and dropped back to fourth and last.

After this debacle, Noel Murless doubted whether the expedition to the States was justified and Captain Moore had to advise it on the ground of expense. The royal colours had never before been raced in America but the Queen saw clearly that to scratch Landau because of his reduced chance of winning would be poor sportsmanship and Her Majesty decided to risk the horse.

Lured by a whiff of toffee, Landau thus duly boarded a transatlantic plane with King of the Tudors as a travelling companion and a box of jam tarts to content them in flight. But before long Noel Murless had to report from the stables in Maryland that the horse had developed a heel infection. This presented a new and incalculable factor. The trouble responded to heel treatment but Landau was set back from exercise.

Then, in the race, the Old Rowley circumstances were curiously repeated. There were seven runners, truly the cream of the Turf, and Landau made a superb start and led them all for the first six furlongs of the mile and a half. Then he yielded to the American favourite, Fisherman, the ultimate winner, and the French Banessa II, falling abruptly behind and finishing last. After this, the Queen concluded his duties and returned him to the National Stud. Shortly afterwards, he was sold for 20,000 guineas to Mr. E. A. Underwood to commence, one may suppose, a luxurious new life of jam tarts in Australia. Incidentally, the Queen's sporting gesture over the International was much appreciated in America and the colours that Landau carried at Laurel Park now rest in the U.S. National Museum of Racing at Saratoga Springs.

12: 'THERE'S BOUND TO BE A LULL'

I

The Queen could look back on 1954 with the satisfaction of the first reigning monarch ever to head a peacetime list of winning owners. Of the twenty-four flat races honoured by the royal silk, nineteen had been won with ten horses and four of the winning two-year-olds at the Lodge had been fully of the Queen's own breeding. At stud now she had in Aureole a stallion, one might dare to hope, the equal of Hyperion. And at the New Year stroke of midnight, when all yearlings become two-year-olds, the stalls occupied by no fewer than fourteen juveniles connoted the Queen's eagerness in experiment as well as the quality of the eighteen Hampton mares.

Yet Her Majesty recognized that the success of her first full racing season as crowned Queen could scarcely be repeated. 'There's bound to be a lull,' she said. At Warren Place the meshwork of contracts around Lester Piggott was ironed out, enabling him to ride as the Queen's first jockey for her National Stud horses while an apprentice rider, Geoff Lewis, was to ride the Stud lightweights. This was high distinction for two youths of eighteen, though the leased three-year-olds — Jardiniere, Annie Oakley, and Whirligig — were only moderate and fresher two-year-old hopes rested merely on three newly leased fillies.

Out early to see the first work of the year on Newmarket Heath, the Queen could watch only four three-year-olds of her own, Alexander, Biscuit, Sierra Nevada, and the flighty Belladonna, a small quartet in contrast with the cavalcade of Boyd-Rochfort juveniles. After luncheon at the Lodge,

159

however, Her Majesty enhanced her day's pleasure by calling on the grey-maned Hyperion at the Woodlands. Fully aware that he was now a quarter-century old, his royal visitor showed that she remembered his preferences by greeting him with a surprise birthday gift of a scrubbed carrot. Even that year the Queen had High Veldt as a promising hopeful by Hyperion–Open Country among her two-year-olds, and Sunburnt Country from the same dam among her yearlings. When a fresh engagement for the two parents was discussed, the Queen suggested with a smiling touch of sentiment that Sundown might be a good name for a foal of either sex. The name was in fact duly bestowed on a colt foal the following year for one of the last sons of Hyperion to figure in active racing.

Later that month the Queen and the Queen Mother also called at Beech House to admire the twenty-year-old Nearco, that remarkable stallion whose son Darius had so often defeated Landau and threatened Aureole. Their Majesties signed the visitors' book kept alongside Nearco's box in the tack-room, praised the stable regimen that had preserved him from as much as a day's illness, talked of the widespread influence of Nearco's brood-mare daughters and mentioned with amusement the difficulty of finding appropriate names for his offspring.

A relevant name as an aid to memory is a practice the Queen likes to maintain in her records. Light-heartedly, at luncheon with one of her trainers one day, she debated the names of some of Hyperion's winning stock with the continual suggestions of sunshine and questioned the remaining possibilities of the Open Country series. The Queen and the Princess Royal each took a share in the forty-share breeding syndicate formed by Sir Victor Sassoon for Pinza, giving them the right to nominate a brood mare. As a variant, the match of Pinza and Open Country had led to the new foal Prairie Song.

In the Court Martial line the new prospect was Above Suspicion by Court Martial–Above Board. Then there had been Spanish Court by Court Martial–Avila, Martial Music by Court Martial–Choral; and Lance-Corporal, a younger brother to Corporal, by Court Martial–Carmen.

An immense amount of ingenuity and wit, indeed, invariably goes into the naming of royal horses. It was one of Captain Moore's duties to submit suggestions to the Queen, but Princess Margaret, the Queen Mother, and Prince Philip were all equally adept at finding names. Often suggestions are mulled among the royal staff and improved upon, or dinner-party guests discuss pertinent new names amid roars of laughter. The foal of Fair Copy and Carmen evoked the name Opera Score. Political wit is evident in Agreement, by Persian Gulf–Northern Hope. Then there was Stenographer (Fair Copy–Saucy Lass), Pall Mall (Palestine–Malapert), Royal Taste (Kingstone–Saucy Lass), Duplicate (Fair Copy–Terracotta), Rosy Glow (Borealis–Terracotta), and occasionally a touch of abstruse scholarship as Alexander by Alycidon–Open Warfare.

The naming of Doutelle, the son of Prince Chevalier and Above Board, led to a pyrotechnical newspaper correspondence from readers anxious to praise Her Majesty's ready wit and historical knowledge and others burdened with fact. The ship that brought Prince Charles Edward to Scotland in 1745 had been named, it was claimed, not Doutelle but *Du Teillay*. On the other hand, the escorting gunboat had been the *Elizabeth* so that this was not the first time Elizabeth and Doutelle had been associated together. Further, the classic *History of the Rebellion of '45* states that the name is also spelled Dutillet and Doutelle, so that it appears the Queen was right.

Meanwhile, the visits to both Hyperion and Nearco reflected the close interest that the Queen was taking in scientific stud life and management following Aureole's assignment. On her birthday weekend the Queen drove down to Gillingham to inspect the National Stud, view the new yearlings, and discuss a dozen problems with Mr. Burrell. Five days later Her Majesty visited the model stables of the Equine Research Establishment in Balaton Lodge, Newmarket, where such fine work is done in veterinary research work and training. The scientists had assumed that the Queen would be more interested in seeing the ponies and horses used for experiment rather than the laboratories, but Her Majesty quickly broke away from the loose box in order to talk to the 'backroom boys' indoors and gain some better idea of their patient, systematic progress.

Eager to explain their work, the physiologists and biologists found it unnecessary to reduce conversation to the elementary terms usual between specialists and laymen. The Queen showed that she had more than a superficial knowledge of genetics and parasitism and such problems as grass infestation and stud infertility. She asked some searching questions of the efficacy of certain glandular products and of the treatment of fractures. Discarding handbag and gloves, she sat down in businesslike fashion to pore over slides and specimens, as eager to learn as any young student.

The Queen was due to go on to the Jockey Club, but this was one of the rare occasions when royal punctuality was in jeopardy. After an hour and a half she was still in the X-ray room, engrossed in comparing photographs. 'Fascinating,' she said, reluctantly breaking away. 'I had no idea the time had gone so quickly.' Since then, she has visited the Station on several occasions, sometimes discussing the problems of her own bloodstock.

By request, the reports of the Station are always sent to Buckingham Palace and Her Majesty has made it known that she follows the work with close interest.

Incidentally, in 1954, the Queen graciously consented to become a patron of the Jockey Club, of the National Hunt Committee and of the Thoroughbred Breeders' Association; yet oddly enough, at the time of writing, the Jockey Club chooses to exclude the Queen as a member. Prince Philip, the Duke of Gloucester and the Duke of Windsor are members, and every reigning monarch since the beginning of the nineteenth century has been a member except Queen Victoria. In this feminist world, with its matriarchal Commonwealth, the Jockey Club still remains one of the exclusive male sanctums from which, save by invitation, women are barred.

Happily, the Queen does not object to the line thus drawn between her patronage as the Sovereign and her interests as a woman racehorse owner and breeder. On the contrary, Her Majesty would no doubt welcome at times a still broader recognition of the distinction between her official activities and her private recreation. Commander Richard Colville, the Queen's Press Secretary, for example, is quick to emphasize that Her Majesty's interests as a racing owner belong essentially to her private life and are thus outside his domain. The involvement of the Sovereign in racing controversy is thereby properly avoided, yet when critical voices are raised, one has the impression that the Queen's days of arduous duty count for too little against her hours of relaxation. Historians will find the criticism of lightweight triviality, one hopes, when dehydrated and dried of contemporary froth. The president of a Methodist Conference once caused deep resentment, so it was reported, when he prefaced his remarks, 'I wish the Queen would not go racing.' But the Queen understood his sincerity and later invited him to one of the famous informal luncheons at Buckingham Palace.

In different vein, a well-meaning Midland cleric sent the Queen a story of two choirboys which he thought might amuse her. Said the first choirboy, 'Now what have we sung the National Anthem for today?' Said the second choirboy, 'I haven't a clue.' Said the first choirboy, 'I suppose it's because the Queen's horse came home first yesterday.'

Naturally a secretary acknowledged the Reverend's letter and politely said that the Queen was much amused. Naturally the friendly parson reported the Queen's pleasure to his parishioners. The next day the story was in the newspapers — and the following day in the Press of the world.

In 1955, however, some agitation surrounded the Queen's attendance at the Grand National. The Aintree event had caused dismay the previous year, when only nine of a field of twenty-nine completed a gruelling race, one horse dropped dead on the course and three others had to be destroyed. As it happened, Peter Cazalet had sent a telegram scratching the Queen Mother's horse a few days before and no royal eyes watched this havoc. But M'as-Tu-Vu was also duly entered for the 1955 National and this time the nomination remained.

The Queen did not fully share her mother's enthusiasm for steeplechasing. Dick Francis once went to ride at Lingfield in a heavy downpour; the parade-ring was practically deserted and three other horses were pitted against the royal runner, but there was the Queen Mother, waiting under the trees. Early in February, however, the Queen accompanied her mother to Hurst Park to see Devon Loch in the New Century Chase, hugging her enthusiastically when Devon Loch won. Undaunted by bitter cold, the Queen and the Queen Mother similarly travelled down to Cheltenham for the National Hunt meeting, changing from their shoes to fur-lined boots to walk doggedly to the paddock. The Queen Mother caught flu and the Queen went to Lingfield alone to report a win for M'as-Tu-Vu a week later. Possibly the Queen had not foreseen the telegrams of protest that arrived at the Palace when it was known she would attend the National, nor the fuss that followed. 'Queen asked, "Do Not Go"', the headlines ran.

On the day, torrents of rain made it appear for a time that the meeting might be abandoned. But the doubts cleared; the Queen, the Queen Mother and Princess Margaret attended as arranged and the royal ladies had the excitement of seeing the royal horse still up after the first circuit and indeed lying second to Sundew. But then he tired and slid to a standstill four fences from home and Quare Times gave trainer Vincent O'Brien a National win for the third year in succession. Moreover, despite the waterlogged course, there were no casualties.

13: ALEXANDER *VERSUS* MELD

I

Throughout all the racing season of 1954, the golden summer of Aureole, the year that first brought Her Majesty into the list of winning owners, probably few of the two-year-old engagements interested the Queen more than the meeting between Her Majesty's Corporal and Lady Zia Wernher's Meld. It was a test, if one may use the phrase, of stripling giants. Corporal was a small yet fine-looking chestnut colt by Court Martial–Carmen who had been first or second in all his seven races to date and had indeed already won three times. Meld was a bay filly by Alycidon–Daily Double whom Captain Boyd-Rochfort, with professional impartiality, dared to pit against the Queen's best.

The Alycidon stock was winning with ever-increasing frequency, already placing him among the top four sires. Yet when Boyd-Rochfort entered Meld in the Foal Stakes he did not really believe he was indulging the rivalry that he knew the Queen and Lady Zia so enjoyed.

On the first autumn day at Newmarket the Queen had her three-year-old filly Festival Light in the Melbourne Stakes, while Lady Zia entered her Alycidon colt Jekyll, and to their owners' amusement both were also-rans. Later that day the Queen vainly had Jardiniere in the Buckenham Stakes while Lady Zia ran Retrial, and neither were in the first three.

The stable expected that Meld would do no better, her essay against Corporal being more in the nature of a trial debut to decide whether she was yet fit to race and perhaps to give her racing confidence. For Meld, at exercise when barely beyond

166

her yearling phase, had suddenly pulled up lame, hopping painfully on three legs, and it was found on return to the stable that she had cracked one of the small bones in her pastern.

It was touch and go whether she would ever stand training.

The Queen invariably enquired after Meld whenever she met Lady Zia. The displacement was not too severe and the split healed cleanly. Gradually the filly was put to light work and the tempo gently increased through the summer until she was put on a three-part-speed gallop and pulled up sound. Admittedly no one expected she could compete within yards of Corporal at Newmarket. To everyone's surprise she finished second, and only two lengths behind.

The Queen and Lady Zia Wernher had good cause to exchange congratulations. Lady Zia impulsively felt she had a possible candidate for the 1,000 Guineas and perhaps the Oaks, while the Queen also had Belladonna, another imposing bay filly by Donatello II–Hypericum, sharing some of Meld's honest characteristics from the same grandsire.

Corporal's prospects might have seemed equally rosy for the 2,000 Guineas, but he was reluctantly discarded from the Queen's considerations. Though speedy, he had no pretensions to stay even a mile, and was sold for shorter track events in California. With her personal string of challengers reduced to four, the Queen concentrated her Derby hopes on Alexander. He was a half-brother of Meld by Alycidon, and his dam, Open Warfare, had bred four winners.

The Queen may have considered that his stoutish look was not to be mistaken for sturdiness, but many were loud in praise of the colt. His abilities had been steadily improving. He had been nowhere in the Rosslyn Stakes on coming out at Ascot but by the September meeting he was second to Sonorous in the Clarence House Stakes, though giving five pounds. Then he won the Duke of Edinburgh Stakes by one and a half lengths, thus earning £1,624 for his owner, the prize that finally placed the Queen at the top of the owners' Est. Unluckily he could not be urged in the Dewhurst and came fifth, some four lengths behind My Smokey, the winner. This defeat notwithstanding, he emerged from the winter on the top of his form for the 2,000 Guineas Trial at Kempton Park.

It was a close race, for the favourite, Our Babu, had the running and held it. But Carr pushed an advantage with Alexander on the far rails almost at the last furlong and won by a clear length and a half.

If anything, Newmarket accordingly intensified the friendly emulation between the Queen and Lady Zia. The Queen evenly weighed her prospects for the 2,000 while Lady Zia had set her heart on the 1,000 fillies' classic. At luncheon in the Royal Box the Queen genially discussed her chances with Lord Porchester, who was running his own colt, Tamerlane. Fate promptly introduced a triangular element, for Our Babu won the 2,000 Guineas from Tamerlane and Alexander was nowhere. Suffering from a splint, Alexander was off colour for the rest of the year.

The next day the Queen had none of her horses engaged, but she spent a happy afternoon as onlooker, arriving soon after one o'clock and remaining to see the Princess Royal's horse Bulbul unplaced in the Somersham. Then, on Guineas Day, the Queen had two runners: her two-year-old Maple Leaf making a debut in the Littleport Stakes and Belladonna opposing Meld in the main event. As a talisman, Her Majesty wore one of the diamond maple-leaf brooches she had been given in Canada, and reasonably effective it proved. Maple Leaf failed only by a length to catch the favourite, Ribambelle, and came in second. Soon the preliminaries for the Guineas found the stands packed and tense. Lady Zia's friends said that they 'hoped she would' and 'hoped she wouldn't' for the Queen's sake; while Lady Zia waited to see whether a long-remembered dream could possibly come true.

One night during the winter she had dreamed she saw Meld hurtling ahead round Tattenham Corner in her colours of green and yellow while a bystander commented: 'That's Meld. She won the 1,000 Guineas and now she's winning the Oaks!'

Daughter of the Grand Duke Michael of Russia, Lady Zia did not believe she has inherited psychic powers, but she was nevertheless impressed. She had once dreamed that Spion Kop was winning the Derby and had backed him on the strength of her vision and seen him win. Coincidence or fuel for the Dunne theory, Meld in due course romped home by two lengths, and while the Queen offered cheerful congratulations on the filly's success, Lady Zia smilingly expressed regrets. For the royal filly, Belladonna, had moped home tenth of twelve.

II

The Queen rounded off her Newmarket week by motoring to Sporte, not far from Sandringham, to watch a meeting of the West Norfolk point-to-point, the first Royal attendance for nearly thirty years. The Duke of Edinburgh was 'on duty' that Saturday, attending the Rugby League Final at Wembley, and the Queen thus entertained her weekend guests. Meanwhile, Belladonna caused anxious consultations, for she was growing more fractious, fully prepared to kick and bite before entering her travelling box. Though Alexander and Jardiniere were both earmarked for the Derby, Murless could not be enthusiastic in his recommendations and the latter was scratched. This decision saw Alexander at Lingfield for the Derby Trial, far from fancied at 30–1. It was Friday, May 13th. Alexander came in fifth of the eight runners and the odds were instantly trumpeted at 100–1.

The following week the European Horse Trials were held in Windsor Great Park. Watching the entries may well have deepened the Queen's doubts of her colt. In the event, he did not run at Epsom.

As usual, the Royal Family were out in force, the royal procession of open cars lustily cheered as it travelled past the stands. Princess Margaret wore a hat of bright cerise and the portent-minded moved with one accord to back Cerise in the first race. Royal racing luck, however, was fully out. Cerise went unplaced. Before the big race the Royal Party moved to the paddocks and stables and again the watchful noted the Queen's obvious interest in Phil Drake. During the parade Her Majesty particularly pointed him out to Prince Philip. Again the Queen was right. Phil Drake streaked as fast as the breeze that so often threatened to unseat Mme Suzy Volterra's big picture-hat.

'I have never seen such a tremendous, such a sensational finishing burst,' said the Queen. Happy to the point of tears, Mme Volterra made her gallant remark that the victory was a memorial to her husband. The Queen, too, was moved…

And so to the Oaks day. Lady Zia Wernher's dream jockey had been clad in new racing silks and obligingly Carr donned a particularly fresh and shiny set. The General Election results were coming in and, in the Royal Box, the Queen was seen listening from time to time to a portable radio. On the course, too, the contest was enhanced once again by a prospective duel between Meld and Belladonna. 'It's a pity I didn't dream about Belladonna,' the Queen said. 'We must wait and see.'

At Tattenham Corner, Meld had a clear lead as in the dream. She was a clear first by six lengths past the judge while Belladonna came home thirteenth and last.

Perhaps then and there a stubborn conviction seized the Queen that she must find a winner, although an historian must be wary in assessing data. Teneretta, the Murless filly, though she had not yet had a race, was the least green of the untried newcomers and offered a suitable last-minute entry for Hurst Park. All the Warren Place jockeys being engaged, Captain Moore tactfully sounded Rae Johnstone. Johnstone said that he was booked, not realizing that he was being asked to ride for the Queen, but the next minute he dashed in the royal racing manager's wake.

'I can easily be here,' he explained.

'Good,' said Captain Moore. 'Then would you like to ride Teneretta for the Queen at Hurst Park?'

Johnstone jumped at the chance, surrendered his bookings at St. Cloud and flew over from Paris. With the Queen Mother's friendly encouragement in the paddock, he longed for a win, but Teneretta could do no better than fourth.

A rail strike now also bedevilled racing, as a newspaper strike had done earlier, and both the Ascot and Newmarket meetings were postponed. The mid-July thunderclouds were brewing before the festive crowds of Royal Ascot could gather as usual and racegoers were never better reminded that royal engagements run to a rigid calendar made up months in advance. The Duke of Edinburgh could not be present, having prior engagements to inspect British Army and Air Force units in Western Germany. There was no Windsor house-party, no procession of elegant landaus.

Fortunately, Jardiniere at last seemed to know what was expected of him when he appeared in the King George V

Stakes. Meld, too, obliged her own mistress by winning the Coronation Stakes by five lengths in a canter.

All afternoon, whenever she went to the parade-ring, the Queen was cheered and applauded. Her one runner was heavily backed, and the cries of 'Come on, The Queen, come on, Jardiniere!' were tumultuous as it streaked past the stands to win by a length and a half. The Queen did not lead in her winner but went to the enclosure and smiled her thanks at Doug Smith before he went to the weighing-in room. 'It was quite satisfactory, wasn't it?' she said to Lord Sefton, and again her horse received the accolade of a specially plucked tuft of grass.

On Gold Vase day Her Majesty could not be present, having arranged a garden party at the Palace. To some this afterwards seemed a move of Providence. The Queen, who so seldom misses a day of Royal Ascot, was thus absent when lightning struck the centre of the course and leapt through the crowd, killing, stunning and injuring, spreading a grim and alarming scene of havoc.

The Queen asked many anxious questions the following day when the catastrophe still cast gloom on the meeting.

On the Saturday all the royal ladies saw the Princess Royal's Va Presco saddled as joint favourite for the Britannia Stakes. Though it was unplaced, the Queen trudged back and forth to the paddock amid the showers or sheltered under the trees, bent on making the best of the afternoon.

Further that summer the young Queen and her husband — she was still not thirty — enjoyed the hospitality of Goodwood House, with the ball at Arundel and Cowdray polo. The Queen saw the unexpected victory of King Bruce in the Stewards' Cup, and next day rejoiced in the thrilling race for Alexander in the Sussex Stakes.

The son of Alycidon had not appeared for three months; his improvement at gallops had been continuous, but then a slight setback kept him on the easy list for some three weeks. The Queen, it was thought, looked doubtfully at her colt in the paddock. But Alexander was soon going like blue blazes and, indeed, rather better, for he passed Blue Blazes at halfway and became the leader. Then Doug Smith came up strongly on My Kingdom and the two spurting runners seemed to cover the last furlong neck and neck.

The word 'photograph' went up on the number-boards, but while the Queen awaited the decision she clearly felt the result would go to My Kingdom and the photo indeed showed him just a neck ahead.

The following day it was the turn of M. Boussac's Elpenor to win the Queen's admiration before the Goodwood Cup, and Maple Leaf gave Her Majesty some excitement by only just losing to a photo finish in the very last race of all.

III

It has long been evident that the Queen takes note of criticism, and Her Majesty was not unaware that her attendance at the St. Leger had provoked some dissidence, although one would have imagined that the undertaking of a long journey to a race meeting during the Balmoral break was surely her own affair. Naturally, the Queen dearly wished to watch Meld accomplish a hat-trick for Lady Zia Wernher if it could be done, and it was therefore made clear that although Her Majesty would attend the St. Leger the visit would be unofficial. The usual Privy Council was notified for Balmoral the following day, and this in reality left the Queen on St. Leger day with a morning free for a new experience.

In courtly language, Her Majesty honoured the Doncaster Yearling Sales with her attendance.

It was the first time in living memory that a reigning monarch had penetrated the somewhat grimy purlieus of the Glasgow Paddocks. At a rumour that the Queen was coming, crowds of women and children gathered from the local streets, at first incredulously and then decisively, for undeniably a corner of the stand was partitioned off, gleaming with fresh paint and abundantly decked with flowers. On the Queen's arrival, the entire crowd of bidders and pressing spectators turned their backs on the auctioneer to applaud Her Majesty and it was a minute or two before the purposeful parades and appraisals of the sale-ring continued.

Mr. Kenneth Watt, one of the Tattersall's partners, sat with the Queen to instruct her in the bidding, and she immediately saw Lot 113 led away after realizing 6,000 guineas. Among other lots Her Majesty saw a Palestine colt quickly sold for 6,300 guineas and she whispered a question or two when a Royal Charger filly did not reach the reserve. To her satisfaction Noel Murless gained a daughter of Big Game for 5,000 guineas and an Alycidon colt fetched 4,600 guineas.

The Queen was so interested, as well as perhaps mystified, by the fate of further lots in the catalogue, that she returned after the racing. The crowd had then thinned and, accompanied by Lord Porchester and Captain Moore, the Queen was able to see some of the yearlings led from the boxes for her inspection.

But of course the big race was the thing, especially as a widespread coughing epidemic had clouded the outcome. Acropolis and Our Babu both coughed their way out of the entries, Phil Drake and Vimy joined these casualties and ultimately no fewer than eleven acceptors were out of the race.

This left Beau Prince, Nucleus and other challengers, with Meld the odds-on favourite. The Queen may well have regretted that she did not have a horse of her own to season the event. And Meld herself had a questionable element, for Captain Boyd-Rochfort, not wishing to tire her, had never fully tried her out over the full length. Moreover, on the eve of the race, in her disinfectant-sprayed box, Meld *coughed…*

She coughed again on St. Leger day, an ominous rasp that made her boy hasten to take her temperature. However, Lady Zia was able to reassure the Queen that apparently all was well. The filly's temperature was normal. Under blue skies, Meld ran her race like the courageous creature she was, though in fact she fell a cough victim the following day.

With Carr up, Piggott on Miss Paget's Nucleus gave her a run all the way. At the end, when Meld had won somewhat lumberingly by three-quarters of a length, Piggott caused consternation. He objected on the score of crossing, but the stewards disallowed him and Meld was upheld.

Meld was thus, I believe, the eighth horse to achieve the classic feat of winning the 1,000 Guineas, the Oaks and St. Leger in all the annals. Returning to Balmoral, delighted for her friend, the Queen could wonder what the remainder of the season had in store. Of her own four three-year-olds of the season, Belladonna had become so jittery that it was six weeks before she could be persuaded to stand still for therapy treatment. Biscuit, having been exasperatingly second and third, was sold to Charles Brook, whereupon he played no better role. Sierra Nevada had been better in performance — with a win and one place — and seemed to have a good chance of winning the Queen Elizabeth Stakes at Ascot. Halfway through the race he was running well against Hafiz II when he abruptly stopped and jolted forward in pain.

Dismounting, Carr found that his mount had broken the off foreleg and there was no choice but a humane end. This was a true disaster, for the horse was only just coming to himself and showed promise of being high-class.

Belladonna, Biscuit, Sierra Nevada, one by one they were whittled away. And that left only one, Alexander.

The Queen put him into the Autumn Select Stakes at Newmarket, where he ran fourth behind Lord Astor's My Smokey, Aberlady (runner-up to Meld in the 1,000 Guineas), and Jaspe. With this improving form, Captain Boyd-Rochfort astutely suggested running him in the Limekiln Stakes a week or two later, and this time Alexander trailed the Astor protagonist all the way to fall by only half a length into second place.

Now, indeed, the prospects of his four-year-old season seemed so benign that the Queen decided he should go on. The lease of Jardiniere was, however, discontinued in accordance with the policy observed for National Stud colts. But Her Majesty continued to keep an eye on her protégé and when he won the Northumberland Plate in the colours of Mr. Tom Lilley the following year, the Queen did not omit to send Noel Murless a congratulatory telegram as the first trainer to win this event three years running.

All the end-of-season decisions were no doubt debated at Luton Hoo, when the Queen and the Duke went there in November for their eighth wedding anniversary. A topical piquancy flavours such occasions. The sixth anniversary had found the young couple frantically busy on the eve of their Commonwealth tour. On the seventh anniversary, amid a plethora that season of State visits and receptions, the Duke had to leave his wife's side to attend the centenary dinner party of the Battle of Balaclava, surely one of the odder royal duties.

Now it was apt that the Queen and her husband should enjoy November 20th at the home of the Wernhers.

Even for more casual visitors this is one of the few great houses of the country with a racing room as well as collections of paintings and porcelain; and the racing cups won by Brown Jack are enshrined not far from the Limoges enamel, the Fra Lippis and Titians. It has been said that racing conversations between the Queen and Lady Zia dove into jargon incomprehensible to the layman and during the evening Meld again won the 1,000 Guineas in a movie.

There was much else to talk about: the not unremarkable achievement of Opera Score, making practically all the running of the Midland Cambridgeshire to win by a head; the decision to race him as a five-year-old; the progress of the budding two-year-olds, among them Atlas and High Veldt, Opalescent and Kolah. There was the engaging possibility of pitting Lady Zia's filly Sonsa against the Queen's Alycidon filly Kantara; the equal rival prospects of the yearlings Doutelle and Cassis, as well as the new hopes for Meld and, of course, Alexander.

Nor need one intrude unduly in supposing that Prince Philip and Sir Harold Wernher were not aloof from any racing conversation. It has been frequently said that Prince Philip did not share the Queen's enthusiasm. He had been known to arrive at Ascot by State landau and skim away in his Lagonda a few minutes later, or to disappear unobtrusively towards the swards of Cowdray after the second race at Goodwood. Yet His Royal Highness was in fact the Vice-President of the British Horse Society, willing to cross England to attend the trials and show jumping at Harewood. He was a member of the Jockey Club, the Jockey Club of France, the Newbury Race Club, and a dozen kindred clubs and organizations. But a spare hour at Ascot one afternoon was typically filled by an exploration of the inside workings of the totalisator. The Prince preferred to miss the big race, discovering how the odds were worked out by calculating machine and how the cash was handled. A punter thrusting a pound-note through the window, crying 'Ten bob each way on Number Four, mate!' discovered himself face to face with the smiling royal visitor. 'I hope it comes up!' Prince Philip chuckled through the wire mesh.

Then there was the occasion when, on being presented with an electrocardiograph by the City of Cambridge, the Queen said smilingly, 'I hope this ingenious machine will be put to good use not many miles from here.' Her audience had not visualized that Prince Philip would borrow the instrument for a vet to check the heartbeats of his polo ponies.

All too often Prince Philip's failure to share all the Queen's racing pleasures was due to sheer lack of time, to his eager desire to fill his leisure with the glowing exercise of physical pursuits, his keenness for active sport rather than a passive role as spectator. Once, while the Queen journeyed to Doncaster, her husband preferred to remain at Balmoral, shooting over the moors with ex-King Michael of Rumania. Prince Philip often toured the stables at Goodwood and Arundel, but he more frequently preferred a trial practice for the annual Arundel cricket match or a 'knock-up' at the nets on the Goodwood lawn. An afternoon's racing that interests the Queen sometimes afforded the Prince an opportunity to fly down to Cowes by helicopter for the sailing. In general, too, Prince Philip placed far more outside engagements on his rota than the Queen was able to do, and usually these duties took him far from the racecourse.

There is, besides, a danger that the Queen's own interest in the breeding and racing of thoroughbred stock can be unduly emphasized.

Emotionally moved by the need for the Hungarian Relief Fund, the Queen decided to part with one of her most prized possessions and gave, for sale on behalf of the fund, her Munnings painting of Aureole, Biscuit and Corporal in cavalcade at the gallops. The Sport of Kings is indeed one of the Queen's favourite pastimes. One rainy afternoon she immersed herself in the massive Zamoyski book of 42,500 pedigrees, looking up first one, then another, of the bloodlines forgetful of all else. 'I found it completely absorbing,' she told the author, Count Stefan Zamoyski, when he was presented to Her Majesty later, and she told him that the green morocco-bound volume was never far from her desk. Yet this preoccupation has only its small recess in the Queen's well-stocked gallery of interests. To everything she undertakes the Queen brings a quality of exceptional painstaking thoroughness, and one does well to remember that this applies to art as well as bloodstock, to the remembrance of past political history as well as tomorrow's Turf achievements.

One can never forget the story told by Professor Albert Richardson, shortly after he became President of the Royal Academy and accompanied the Queen round an exhibition of eighteenth-century masters. 'I had intended to tell her about each picture,' he said. 'Instead she told me, and I did nearly all the listening.'

He went on: 'She is amazing. She talked about the derivation of the exhibits and I could not add to her knowledge. An interior of Buckingham Palace was shown in one of the paintings. She pointed to a clock in the picture and told me: "That was there in Queen Charlotte's time. It is still there."'

This incident surely sets in perspective any improper exaggeration of Her Majesty's racing zeal, though it has perhaps been stressed unavoidably in this volume.

IV

Although Alexander continued to engage Her Majesty's affectionate interest, the Queen was not too dismayed when, on his first outing as a four-year-old — on April 21st, 1956, at Hurst Park — he failed to give her a suitable thirtieth birthday recognition and was nowhere in the Victoria Cup. Her Majesty merely agreed with Captain Boyd-Rochfort that the entry for the colt in the Great Jubilee at Kempton Park should stand and this decision proved effective. Without undue weight, Alexander was then second to Tudor Jinks and ahead of High Bhan and the previous year's Royal Hunt Cup winner, Nicholas Nickleby. The Queen felt at once that her horse might well win the 1956 Royal Hunt Cup.

The Hunt Cup is, of course, a handicap, with the chances of each horse equalized by the handicapper, setting a difficult task to the forecasters, but this time the pundits hedged and guarded their opinions with special care. The first six horses of the Jubilee were again in opposition, but a ten pound penalty on Tudor Jinks seemed to put him out of court. Alexander was meeting Nicholas Nickleby on two pound better terms and High Bhan on terms one pound less favourable. Then there was Lady Ursula Vernon's Jaspe, who had won over the course and the distance. Nicholas Nickleby, the previous year's winner, seemed promising; but in more than a century only one horse had ever won the Royal Hunt Cup twice. On balance Alexander was proclaimed the favourite at the call-over and yet no clear favourite had won since 1910. Here indeed was food for weighty argument. When Alexander appeared in blinkers, many racegoers felt he was not half as blinkered as they.

Looking back at that Royal Hunt Cup day, I remember thinking that the Queen had seldom looked so attractive, so summery and gay and expectant. In the paddock she told Carr that she wanted to watch the running purely on the form and gave him strict instructions that he was on no account to touch Alexander with the whip. Riding therefore solely with hands and heels, Carr gave Alexander his head after the first two hundred yards and he quickly went into the lead on the stand side.

On the far side Nicholas Nickleby made way for a group that included Blue Robe, Kenmore and Jaspe. The excitement was intense when Johnstone on the far rails took Jaspe into the lead. 'I could see Jaspe coming up out of the corner of my eye,' said Carr. 'I was never more than a length in front.' And then a great sigh of puzzlement swept the crowds, for no one could be sure whether Jaspe or Alexander had won, separated as they were by the green width of the turf.

Johnstone without further ado took his horse straight to the appointed place for the runner-up, but this could have been no more than a good-mannered gesture. The crowd cheered for Carr, but he looked apprehensive and shrugged his shoulders.

Although the Queen smiled, she imagined she had lost; and the judge seemed to take his time with the photo. Never was there such a tense, expectant four minutes. Then the loudspeakers announced, 'First, No. 3.' This confused the crowd a little, but the Queen immediately bubbled with laughter.

Alexander had won. 'Bad luck,' Her Majesty immediately commiserated with Lady Ursula Vernon. 'It was very close.' And Lady Ursula could not help but agree with a pressman who suggested that if she had won it would have been the most unpopular win of the year.

Alexander next went for the Eclipse Stakes, probably the most valuable event staged at Sandown, but he showed no spirit against Hafiz II or Tropique, the French winner, and dawdled home sixth in a field of eight. Finally, in a farewell appearance at York, he straggled home in a handicap race very much with the field. These defeats did not matter. Alexander had made his conquests. When the Queen disposed of him at the Newmarket December sales, the proper fame of his achievement was gauged by his purchase for stud in South Africa at 9,500 guineas, the top price of the day.

Unhappily, Alexander broke his neck in an accident after his second service. But he had won the immortal laurels of racing glory in capping Choir Boy's feat and enabling the Queen to win the Royal Hunt Cup for the second time.

14: HIGH VELDT AND ATLAS

I

Of all the lengthy string of fourteen two-year-olds in training for the Queen at Freemason Lodge in 1955, only six runners survived into the group of intended three-year-old challengers of 1956. This was nevertheless a high and satisfying level for so discriminating a client, and it was a buoyant Captain Boyd-Rochfort who made his New Year round of Atlas and High Veldt, Medici, Opalescent, Kantara and Spanish Court. When asked about the royal horses, he admitted to having better hopes for 1956 than he could remember having for 1955. Behind this guarded admission there lay indeed the prospect that the Queen's horses might help to lift him to the top of the winning trainers' list for the third year running.

The week before the Queen undertook her journey to Nigeria she visited both Warren Place and Freemason Lodge with the Queen Mother and Princess Margaret. Increasingly, while public formality intensified, the Queen was to enjoy nothing better than the informality of these visits, changing into her brogues at the back of the car, pottering around a stable-yard or donning a dustcoat to watch the gallops on the Heath. Noel Murless had brought forward only Teneretta and Vettura, but his royal string of eight two-year-olds compared agreeably with the new Boyd-Rochfort two-year-old batch of nine.

Pleased with the look of the Dante newcomer, Carrozza, the royal ladies went on to luncheon at the Lodge. The conversation bubbled with the season's coming plans. High Veldt, for instance, in the King George VI and Queen

183

Elizabeth and then in the St. Leger — what a coup! (The two races together would be worth £36,000.) Then Atlas in the Derby, Spanish Court in the Oaks, not forgetting Alexander in the Royal Hunt Cup, so the giddily enticing prospects ran. One can imagine that Captain Boyd-Rochfort balanced these bright hopes in his courtly way and he no doubt wished the Queen Mother all good luck with her really compelling Grand National prospect, Devon Loch. Seldom had there been a season so well covered by auspicious plans. Bruce Hobbs, Captain Boyd-Rochfort's assistant, felt at this time that the Captain had a Derby win in sight. But would it be with Atlas or High Veldt? This was the razor-edged problem for decision.

High Veldt had been quite a problem child. The son of Hyperion by Open Country was in fact the mare's first surviving foal, her earlier by Kingstone having died. And High Veldt had at first shown himself one of those excessively troublesome horses of high breeding who prefer to rear on two legs rather than run on four.

'This is a dog. You can do nothing with him,' the trainer told a consultant.

As his visitor realized, this implied no more than that he was handling an animal bred to fine pitch, a horse requiring the utmost finesse in training and in the selection of races. Such a thoroughbred usually presents a trainer with his greatest headaches and often recompenses him with his greatest triumphs. There were times when High Veldt could not be persuaded to start at gallops, let alone to match his strength. Resentful at times of bystanders, bit, bridle, saddle, the touch of a hand, he evinced the prima donna qualities that are so often the sign of a classic star.

Once set to a gallop he would wander out, or else assume a 'couldn't care less' air of extreme vapidity. Yet High Veldt, the stable knew, could prove another Aureole.

As a two-year-old he first gained interest by running fourth to Idle Rocks, Monterey and Ratification in the Woodcote Stakes at Epsom. It was true that he straggled no less than six lengths behind Ratification, who was in turn separated by three and a half lengths from the winner. But Idle Rocks and Ratification were much-discussed rivals, and the latter was already being acclaimed, despite setbacks, as one of the best two-year-olds of the season.

High Veldt's evident anxiety to catch up with him betokened spirit. With less incentive, High Veldt was nowhere next time out at Newbury. But then the Soltykoff Stakes came along at Newmarket; and the Queen, sailing round the western coasts of Britain aboard the *Britannia*, received the pleasant news that High Veldt had a win.

This looked propitious. Earlier the same afternoon the Royal colours had a defeat when Annie Oakley, the National Stud filly, was beaten in the New Falmouth Stakes. Now the Soltykoff showed that High Veldt was responding to nervous system therapy as Belladonna, Angelola at stud and Spanish Court had all done that season. Not that the win had been easy. The favourite, Royal Slipper, had led most of the way and it looked at one time that High Veldt would get squeezed in the crowd. But perhaps this angered the colt. Certainly he responded well when Carr asked and galloped resolutely up the hill to win by two lengths. From the Queen's point of view, the sole misfortune was that Mrs. Murless's Abernant filly, Riccal, was beaten to third.

Best of all, however, in October the two-year-old High Veldt won the Houghton Stakes by half a length from Chantelsey with Idle Rocks four lengths further away, third. This was exhilarating for Idle Rocks, having won the Gimcrack Stakes, had been firm favourite and had led for some way. But then he faltered with flapping ears while High Veldt arrived so untired at the post that he was voted a natural stayer.

Quietly and decisively the moves were thus made that anticipated the royal coup at Ascot and Town Moor. Meanwhile, Atlas also fitted excitingly into the jigsaw. By Djebel out of Young Entry, this chestnut colt had been delayed in his debut by rheumatic treatment, and the stable deferred his coming out till the Sandwich Stakes at Ascot. Very creditably Atlas then came in fourth, showing his heels by five lengths to the rest of the field plodding far behind. Three weeks later he ran in the Dewhurst, facing such opposition as Ratification and the Dante colt Dacian. The latter had attracted a great deal of attention as a stayer and Ratification was conceding weight. But the Queen's horse challenged in the Dip, brisked into an extremely fast race and nearly had it. Dacian indeed won only by a head from Atlas, with a further clear length from Ratification. Since this news reached the Queen only the day after High Veldt's Houghton victory, Her Majesty was delighted.

The twelfth and last success of the Queen's 1955 racing season had been reserved, however, for little Spanish Court. Sierra Nevada's half-sister had her ups and downs. Indeed the fitting of racing plates was more commonly a signal for the desponds rather than the crests. She had twice been runner-up but never a winner. Then, in the Humberstone Fillies' Plate at Leicester, when flat racing was all but ended, she not only made the running all the way but gave Midland racegoers a further taste of royal style by establishing a new course record.

II

The Queen found her energies absorbed early in 1956 by the triumphs of the Nigerian tour, and for a week in March she gained brief respite cruising with Prince Philip in the waters of Corsica. To return to the chills of Britain seemed dismal, but the Queen was bent on finding time for Devon Loch's National, among other engagements, and she returned to London six days beforehand eager to hear all the training news.

The Queen has never hugged and kissed her mother with greater vivacity in public than on an occasion when Devon Loch won a Hurst Park steeplechase through a quagmire. And only the month before the Grand National, mother and daughter went to Cheltenham to watch Devon Loch's spring debut.

'The horse may not be quite ready today, ma'am,' Mr. Cazalet warned the Queen. 'For, of course, the Grand National is the real objective.'

'Yes,' said Her Majesty with a smile. 'But there's no harm in picking this one up on the way.'

In fact, Devon Loch finished third at Cheltenham. But he had come from nearly last on the first circuit and was still running tirelessly on at the close. Many people who watched Devon Loch that day felt sure they were watching the National winner. He had been bought for Queen Elizabeth the Queen Mother five years before when he had done no more than win a two-mile flat race for amateur riders, the only race he had ever entered. Now he had come over all the hurdles of novice chases and handicap races, not just a superb brown horse of commanding colour, perfectly groomed, carrying Royal silk, but an intelligent creature that seemed to radiate the magnetism of stardom. He may indeed have played some part for a time in the subtle nuances of Soviet power politics, for M.

187

Malenkov, Stalin's short-term successor, had expressed a wish to see the Grand National while touring Britain and the Hammer and Sickle flew from a flagpole nearly opposite the Royal Box. Nor should it be forgotten that two riders, Arthur Freeman and Dick Francis, both carried the Queen Mother's blue and buff stripes and black velvet cap. In the paddock the Queen, the Queen Mother, Princess Margaret and the Princess Royal admired the rippling fitness of not only Devon Loch but also M'as-Tu-Vu.

At one time, early in this never-to-be-forgotten Grand National, M'as-Tu-Vu was leading. Though slighter than his companion, he completed the first circuit despite the usual mêlée of sprawling horses; and at the stands the royal ladies had the immense satisfaction and excitement of seeing their two favourites still running together, still in action.

In open country again, M'as-Tu-Vu was at the twentieth of the thirty jumps, the ditch and fence, before he fell. Meanwhile Devon Loch sailed on, as it seemed to Dick Francis, like a horse in a dream, meeting every fence perfectly, passing horse after horse.

Then the appalling collapse less than fifty yards from the winning post, every fence jumped, with the practical certainty that the race was won by many lengths… Suddenly the last stride, Devon Loch's legs splaying outwards as he fell flat on his belly… The next moment Devon Loch was passed by every horse remaining in the field and the race was over.

The Queen put a distracted hand to her forehead. The Queen Mother's hand went to her heart. Characteristically the royal ladies immediately thought of the rider's disappointment and, indeed, the Queen Mother and Princess Margaret went in search of Francis for a time until he could be found and brought to the Royal Box. 'It was such a beautiful race,' the

Queen Mother tried to console him, resignedly. 'But that's racing, I suppose.'

Later, the Queen and her mother went to see Devon Loch, trying to solve the riddle that has remained unanswered ever since. They found him reasonably fresh and quite unharmed. What had happened to him? Had some lack of oxygen or a sudden cramp deprived him for an instant of movement? Had he hit a turf slip? It was never found. Had he been startled by a side glimpse of the water-jump? Or had he been jerked convulsively backward by the cheers that greeted him, a frightening, shattering wave of sound?

The baffling questions will never be settled, but there remains a footnote. Many casual racegoers, I find, imagine that this brave and noble horse never raced again. But seven months later he reappeared in the Bulcote Hurdle at Nottingham, his first race since the National, in a race that should surely be for ever linked with his Aintree breakdown. Turning up the long straight, he was well behind the leaders, Northern King, Twin Star and Misty Devil, and appeared to have small hope of winning.

But let the rest of the story be told in the commanding words of Queen Elizabeth the Queen Mother's racing records, which I am graciously permitted to quote: 'Even after jumping the second last flight, his chance seemed remote. He then started such a run as could hardly be imagined, especially for a four-mile chaser. Though Northern King (destined to be the crack two-mile Novice Chaser) led over the last, and was still in front sixty yards from the post, Devon Loch passed him so fast that he won by two lengths.'

III

On the flat, the first royal victory of 1956 came when the

Queen took a Saturday afternoon off at Hurst Park and saw High Veldt win the 2,000 Guineas Trial Stakes from the odds-on favourite, Rustam. This was indeed an auspicious beginning; for Rustam was considered by many a horse of the year. Unbeaten in his three races as a two-year-old, he had already won £10,000 for his owner, Lady Wyfold, and was in the top six of the Free Handicap. Watched by the TV cameras, the Boyd-Rochfort stable-lad, Fussey, was rightly beaming with pride as he led High Veldt to the unsaddling enclosure. Unfortunately, High Veldt was struck out of his major classics the previous winter, and he was left in neither the 2,000 Guineas nor the Derby. Her Majesty clearly recognized that High Veldt, though so like his sire Hyperion in looks, was not another Aureole and she recognized, too, the shattering strain that the ardours of Epsom can sometimes inflict on smaller horses, and so High Veldt's future was not too deeply questioned.

That weekend, too, the Queen hoped for a double, for Piggott rode Teneretta in the 1,000 Guineas Trial at Kempton Park on Monday, but the National Stud filly alas came in only fifth. Nor was this reversal of royal fortunes much improved when Atlas as the favourite opposed Monterey in the Blue Riband Stakes at the Epsom April meeting and came in third behind Monterey and Tudor Era. Among other equine interests at this time, the Queen saw the Badminton Horse Trials and went down to Ascot with the Queen Mother to inspect the improvements. But the daunting mystery of the Derby still remained.

At the Queen's wish, Atlas was sent up to Chester for a try-out in the Dee Stakes over the Derby distance in early May. He not only took the lead half a mile out but won comfortably by two lengths from French Beige, from whom he was receiving five pounds and ten lengths from Ski Maid, third. This result was no surprise to Captain Boyd-Rochfort, who admitted that the trial over the distance had been the thing but it was unfortunately the last satisfaction from Atlas for some time.

The Derby clashed with the State visit to Sweden, during which the Queen so much enjoyed the equestrian events of the Olympic Games, and so Her Majesty was not at Epsom. Instead, the Queen Mother and Princess Margaret watched in the rain and saw the rout of Atlas to fifth place behind the French-trained favourite Lavandin, the French-trained outsider Montaval, and the Irish horse Roistar.

Lord Astor's Hornbeam was fourth, a head from Atlas, and matching the form Monterey came sixth. Was it Atlas's fault? Was the royal horse bunched? There was a large field of twenty-seven that year. Mercer reported that Hornbeam had been hopelessly boxed in down the hill and Atlas may well have shared that fate, for he lacked speed at the start and was late in joining the leaders. The inquest is of no avail. It took only a few days in May and June to disperse all the rosy royal dreams of a coup. Except, of course, that 'it might be all right at Ascot'.

IV

Returning from Sweden, the Queen drove direct from London Airport to Windsor for her Ascot house-party. For the first time, that year, the five landaus of the royal procession drove up the new straight mile, past the enlarged and liberated Royal Enclosure and the new Queen's Lawn. With Alexander, Atlas and High Veldt all engaged, the Queen had three runners whom she had watched from the foaling box, yet there was probably no race more intricate and appealing than the St. James's Palace Stakes on the opening afternoon. It brought into competition with High Veldt both the 501 surprise winner of the 2,000 Guineas, Gilles de Retz, and the French 2,000 Guineas winner, Buisson Ardent, as well as the old challengers, Ratification and Monterey. Moreover, High Veldt had not appeared since the Classic Trial at Thirsk when he found himself pitted against Ratification and won. Now there was also Pirate King, a horse Atlas had managed to pass — with Monterey and Buisson Ardent — in the Derby. All these rivals raised anew the challenging comparison between High Veldt and Atlas. Should High Veldt, smaller but perhaps a shade better bred, have been the Derby horse? Should Atlas — sired by M. Boussac's Djebel in the Herod line — have been trained instead for the top prize of the King George V and Queen Elizabeth Stakes?

These questions, so clear-cut beforehand, seemed scarcely better answered when the race was won. The finish saw four horses bunched so close that only the camera could resolve the tangle — and the line showed Pirate King winning by inches from Buisson Ardent with inches again from Ratification and from High Veldt fourth. The crowds had no occasion to cheer a royal winner, a loyal pleasure reserved for the following day when, as we have seen, Alexander scooped the Royal Hunt Cup. It should have been Atlas's turn on Thursday in the King Edward VII Stakes, but he ran notably out of turn, coming home somewhere with the field.

The Queen none the less was pleased. She had pinned her masterplan on High Veldt and her confidence seemed correct. If any horse in her ownership could wrest the £28,000 prize of the King George VI and Queen Elizabeth Stakes from the Italian favourite, Ribot, unbeaten in thirteen races, it was High Veldt. The fabric of the intended royal coup had been tattered by the winds of racing chance, but the essential skeins remained. Though Her Majesty had no further runners at Royal Ascot, she watched the parades in the paddock with renewed interest, perhaps to cast a speculative eye on Chantelsey, who had finished the 2,000 Guineas well in front of Buisson Ardent. (It was at this meeting, incidentally, that a woman clutched the Queen's arm, to be sharply pushed away by the Duke of Gloucester.) On Saturday, as usual, the Queen arrived informally with the Queen Mother and Princess Margaret to see Sir Winston Churchill's horse, Le Pretendant, in the Churchill Stakes. Yet perhaps food for thought remained in the close duel of the four-year-olds Kurun and Daemon in the Hardwicke Stakes, both of whom were to run in the 'King and Queen'.

In the month dividing Royal Ascot from the summer meeting, the stable reports continued favourably. At gallops, High Veldt did a good deal better than Zarathustra, the Gold Cup winner. His starting behaviour was exemplary. Meanwhile there were whispers that the unbeatable Ribot had slightly injured a leg in galloping, whispers speedily put to flight as soon as he arrived at Ascot and achieved an effortless practice run round the course.

When the meeting opened, High Veldt *versus* Ribot was a feast reserved for the second day, and royal horses were scattered through the programme like plaques on green baize. A State visit from King Feisal of Iraq ended just in time to allow Her Majesty to attend the opening day. And promptly the Queen's Spanish Court finished as runner-up in the first race. The Red Oaks Stakes, wresting second place when close to home, while the Hampton-bred Doutelle — a two-year-old making his debut as an outsider — next won the Granville Stakes by a handsome three lengths.

These were favourable omens. Nevertheless, another royal debutante, the National Stud's Great Birnam, just missed a place in the Virginia Water Stakes and the Queen's fourth runner that day, the Alycidon filly Kantara, was merely sixth in the Cranbourne Chase Stakes. At her private stable-yard at the top of the paddock, the Queen visited High Veldt in his billet to find him in fine fettle. Though the going would be soft, this never deterred him, but other factors remained inscrutable. The weight-for-age scale favoured the three-year-olds against the four-year-old Ribot. Four-year-olds seemed to have little success in the 'King and Queen'. On the other hand, Ribot's sire Tenerani had won the race at four years old when it was first founded and so had Aureole.

Truly this was a race fit to set before so intensively expert an owner as the Queen. Here was the barrel-chested bay wonder horse Ribot; the winner of the Belgian Derby, Todrai; the intriguing Roistar, first British horse in the English Derby, and Chantelsey, whose not least claim to fame was that he had once passed a post half a length from High Veldt; and many others. Going down to the paddock, the Queen, the Queen Mother, Princess Margaret, and the Princess Royal congratulated Sir Winston Churchill, whose horse, Collusion, had just won the Rosslyn Stakes. Then they had scarcely returned to the Royal Box than there came a moment of high excitement.

The horses were under starter's orders when Todrai suddenly charged the tapes, unseated his jockey and bolted. Cantering along the course, he must have reminded the Queen vividly of the incident ten years before when Hypericum had bolted before the 1,000 Guineas at Newmarket. Like Hypericum, Todrai made for the car park, where he was firmly caught and brought back after a long delay. The other horses, waiting at the start, needed all their riders' skill to ease the nervous tension. And the unhurt jockey had no sooner remounted Todrai than another instant of tension must have reached the Queen as she watched through her glasses. *High Veldt reared.*

It was this old trick, seldom seen now for months, that had so often caused a bad start and lost him races. Treatment by Charles Brook, and the skill of Captain Boyd-Rochfort in pairing him to Opera Score as a working companion, seemed to have eradicated the habit. Yet High Veldt reared…

Then they were off. Daemon and Todrai took up the running, with Ribot and Chantelsey close behind. One horse was left by lengths, but Carr had High Veldt drawing forward. At the foot of the hill Ribot almost lost the race in the seconds when he floundered in a bad patch of unaccustomed soft ground. At the final bend it was, however, Todrai and Ribot, the failing Chantelsey and High Veldt. Then Carr shot High Veldt forward nearer the rails.

In his many races in Europe Ribot must often have heard deafening cheers. But surely he pricked his ears higher than usual at the tremendous tumult that greeted the last yards' battle with High Veldt, Todrai falling back. The fabulous powers of Ribot could not be eclipsed, however, though High Veldt strongly challenged. The Italian horse won with High Veldt second by two lengths.

This must have been one of the greatest defeats of the Queen's racing career, yet a few minutes later she was congratulating the Marchese Incisa della Rocchetta with undiminished enthusiasm. 'How wonderful to have such a horse!' she exclaimed, warmly shaking his hand. And already, with zestful resilience, she had decided that High Veldt should certainly run in the St. Leger and have another try for the King George VI and Queen Elizabeth the following year.

V

And so to Goodwood, where formality always disperses amid the breezy hilltops of the Sussex Downs and the Queen may have hoped to relax with her friends or, at least, not to disappoint them. The times were anxious, for President Nasser had seized the Suez Canal and Her Majesty had enquired whether she should remain in London, but had been reassured. As it happened, this led to the story, surely put about not without malice, that the Queen had signed a call-up at the races.

In fact, during Goodwood Week, a Proclamation calling out the Army Reserve became necessary, and the Queen properly agreed to approve the draft text at the earliest possible moment. As soon as it was ready, the document was therefore hurriedly taken to her private rooms in the Duke of Richmond's box. The next day the Proclamation was formally signed at a Privy Council at Arundel Castle, where Her Majesty was in residence as the guest of the Duke and Duchess of Norfolk. Wherever she had been, the Queen could have done no more.

Inevitably the Suez events shadowed the Goodwood racing. But the Duke of Edinburgh was sufficiently impressed by Doutelle to wait on the opening day to see him in the last race, the New Ham Foal Stakes, when the young colt came in to a photo-finish. Then there was the friendly rivalry on the last day when Lady Zia Wernher thought that her horse Sonsa might win the Nassau Stakes while the Queen felt equally sure that the victory could go to her filly Kantara.

Both horses were trained in the Boyd-Rochfort stable. Neither were selected on the marked card service. Lady Zia and the Queen were both intensely excited when the race began and burst into laughter together at the end. In the field of nine, both Sonsa and Kantara were unplaced.

VI

Every trainer is familiar with the horse who breaks down after a particularly arduous race so that he becomes unfit for further service except to pass on the qualities of speed and stamina in his bloodline at stud. Was High Veldt such a horse? Was he wrecked by the rigours of the two-mile 'King and Queen' covering the ground, as he did, in better time than Aureole?

Through the August torpors Captain Boyd-Rochfort watched the colt anxiously. When Carr took him over ten furlongs he seemed as sprightly as ever. Both High Veldt and Atlas were originally entered for the St. Leger but Atlas retreated at the first acceptance and High Veldt was soon installed favourite.

As before, the Queen travelled from Balmoral for the St. Leger, arriving by train and spending the morning at the yearling sales. This time, however, Her Majesty was no mere spectator, but had set her heart on making a purchase or two with the ultimate intention of introducing fresh blood to Hampton. After watching some thirty lots sold, she started out for the stables to inspect the waiting horses with Lord Porchester and Captain Moore, from time to time studying her catalogue intently. But unluckily so many people crowded after her and the police had such difficulty in clearing a path that buyers soon had the impression that the Queen had perhaps cut short her visit.

In any event, it was not a lucky day, for High Veldt clearly found the St. Leger beyond him, lagging when half a mile from home, and opinions were that he did well to finish fifth. Not to waste her time, the Queen returned to the Park Paddocks and spent another hour watching the yearling sales. By now the crowds had dispersed and no particular interest seemed to attach to a Sledmere filly by Petition–Danse d'Espoir knocked down to the London Bloodstock Agency for 4,100 guineas, nor to a Middleton Stud filly by Luminary out of Whoa Emma bought by the same firm for 1,150 guineas. Even the agents did not realize they were shopping for the Queen of England.

The Queen had to return to Balmoral to meet Mr. Menzies, the Prime Minister of Australia, after his Suez talks, and so she did not see Atlas's thrilling win in the Doncaster Cup. This two-mile two furlong event is, of course, one of the oldest and most strenuous in the calendar and it found Atlas engaged in a series of ding-dong battles all the way. First one horse, then another, alternated for the lead while Atlas still made headway until, three furlongs from the post, the Queen's horse at last gained the lead from By Thunder, the Ebor Handicap winner. What was more, he held the lead, steadily increasing, until he hurtled past the post to win by six lengths amid a tumultuous welcome.

He was the fourth Boyd-Rochfort horse to win the Doncaster Cup and certainly the smallest. On this showing he could have won the St. Leger. To judge by the King George VI and Queen Elizabeth Stakes, High Veldt could have won the Derby. But the skeins were twisted and the tactical placings were destined to be for ever debated.

There remained only the tag-end of the year. At Kempton Park in October the Queen hoped to see a double with Kantara and the two-year-old Mulberry Harbour, but both were unplaced. In six races the luckless Kantara had never won once. Next day Her Majesty was again present to see High Veldt in the Cumberland Lodge Stakes. Ridden by Breasley, he was in better form and ran second to Sir Winston Churchill's redoubtable Le Pretendant. A week earlier, in this constant duet, Atlas had failed to win the Jockey Club Stakes, falling third to Kurun and Cardington King with only seven runners. Medici, too, an endearing colt by Donatello II–Hypericum, made a long-delayed three-year-old first appearance at Newmarket only to prove an also-ran. But all these mediocre events were replaced by radiant delight when a message reached the Queen in Cumberland, shortly after she had opened the first atomic power station, reporting that Medici had won a race at Newmarket by four lengths.

The Queen is always prepared to take infinite pains with backward or ailing horses. Nothing is too much trouble. One horse, slightly lame in the left shoulder, was sent away to Seaford because it was thought that the sea air and salt water bathing might suit him. Another with slight muscular trouble at the end of his racing career was sent to Miss Norah Wilmot, the Berkshire specialist in the advanced electrical treatment of horses, in order that he might be fit and happy in retirement. Opalescent, Miner's Lamp, Devon Loch and other royal horses have all passed through Miss Wilmot's sympathetic hands. Concerned lest her Buckingham Palace carriage horses were not getting enough fresh air and sunshine, the Queen arranged a rota system enabling them to enjoy the clean air of Windsor for a few days at a time.

'If ever I am Queen there must be no riding on Sundays. Horses should have a rest, too,' the little Lilibet had said years ago. Now, as Queen, touring an agricultural show, she recognized a pit pony she had seen two years before when one of its legs was bandaged after a kick from a stray horse and promptly remembered that she had seen it when injured and enquired if it were fully recovered.

Of all the invalids none was as endearing as Medici. He was an extraordinarily nervous horse; a big backward giant who took a long time to come to hand. Captain Boyd-Rochfort and Bruce Hobbs lavished their utmost skill and patience on him, Charles Brook was called in, and his stable-girl, Ann Kidman, never spared herself in humouring him, gently cajoling him and making him happy. When he at last entered a race, successfully able to withstand the noise and movement of the crowds, the Queen felt that a triumph had been achieved comparable with and eclipsing her first victory with Astrakhan. When the floppy Medici won his second race, she was overjoyed.

Unhappily, his story has a tragic ending. The outlook was bright. The care lavished for so long on the timid colt was, it seemed, on the eve of being fully rewarded. In 1956 the Queen had twenty-three horses running in eighty-eight races. They appeared at Leicester and Great Yarmouth, Newcastle, Brighton and Thirsk, as well as the classic venues. They ranged from the spirited challenges of the five-year-old gelding Opera Score to the Murless wins with Teneretta and his royal two-year-olds Deck Tennis and Anthracite.

Altogether, thirteen of the Queen's horses won at least one race. Medici was the thirteenth horse in this winning list. And one November morning, rearing at some misty terror, he slipped over backwards and broke his back.

VII

The riddle of High Veldt lingered long into 1957. His first main objective, it was decided, should be the Coronation Cup, for his owner was still primarily anxious to know how he would fare over the Epsom mile and a half Derby course. Besides, the Coronation had been won by Aureole before going on to win the King George VI and Queen Elizabeth

Stakes and, in testing High Veldt as a four-year-old, such echoes were not to be lightly ignored. In April the John Porter Stakes at Newbury was tried out on the way, one good reason being the rival entry of China Rock, who was also entered for the 'King and Queen'. But High Veldt unfortunately came in fourth, not only falling behind China Rock, the winner, but also Shikar II and Court Command, never approaching his Ascot style.

The Coronation Cup was won by the French-bred Fric in two seconds faster time than the Derby High Veldt had missed the previous year, and the stopwatch found High Veldt lying third to Fric, with Gilles de Retz, Pirate King and other rivals left behind. Next, in this exacting process of timing, High Veldt was entered in the Hardwicke Stakes over the Ascot one and a half miles. He was in savage mood and this was one of the few occasions when the Queen came near to being hurt by one of her own horses. Her Majesty went to the stables to see High Veldt saddled and her attention was momentarily preoccupied when suddenly High Veldt threw up his heels and lashed out.

'Take care, take care!' the Princess Royal cried, pulling the Queen aside.

Court Command, one of the other runners, was brought up as a walking companion, but immediately he too pranced and refused to move. It took some extreme coaxing on the part of both the Boyd-Rochfort and Murless lads before the two waltzers could be quietly walked. Then, in the race, High Veldt came in third to Fric, though four lengths behind Pirate King, the runner-up.

Had he a possible hope of winning the King George VI and Queen Elizabeth Stakes, against Fric and his old rival Todrai; Montaval, the runner-up in the 1956 Derby; Tissot, an Italian white hope, and the rest? To pare the sad story, instead of the sunny victory she once dreamed of seeing, the Queen saw High Veldt wallowing in a mud bath, for a downpour of tropical intensity almost wrecked the course before the race. It was, of course, Montaval's win … and High Veldt came in last.

His run with Ribot may indeed have demanded too much, for he never again raced with the same zest. When he next appeared at Ascot Heath it was to come in sixth of a field of seven; and in the Select Stakes at Newmarket barely three weeks later he was sixth and last. His best successes nevertheless showed that he bore all the hallmarks of his breeding, and in 1958 he was sold to the Birch brothers, two of the leading breeders of South Africa, for £10,000.

15: CARROZZA AND DOUTELLE

I

Among the diversions of the racing columns early in the flat-racing season of 1957, the Queen could have been regaled by the royal chase of the cheese. This somewhat mystical affair concerned the initial appearance of Atlas as a four-year-old in the Chester Cup, a race that includes among its perquisites the presentation of a fifty-pound Cheshire cheese as well as a piece of plate and about £2,000 in cash. In all the annals this race has never been won by a leading monarch and this may have been a royal consolation when Atlas came in not first but second, six lengths behind the 1955 Cesarewitch winner Curry, who had led readily all the way.

Happily for his reputation Atlas did better when he travelled to Haydock Park a week later. Pall Mall, the two-year-old colt by Palestine–Malapert, made a sensational first appearance that day by winning the first race (for two-year-old maidens) by five lengths. Atlas then carried off the Haydock Park Stakes in record time; and finally Carr, changing with alacrity from one royal mount to another, completed the hat-trick by winning the last race with the Migoli–Northern Hope filly Might and Main.

This was the first treble the Queen ever achieved in her racing ownership. In 1956 her stake winnings had reached the ultimate total of £16,530, but already, by the end of this afternoon, she had reached £12,500 in eight races. It was the first time the royal colours had embellished Haydock Park in over thirty years and it was, of course, a fine cap-feather for Atlas. Yet, sad to say, it was the last race he ever won. When he

203

ran a few days later in the Combe Stakes at Sandown, China Rock snatched the victory by a neck.

Next the Winston Churchill Stakes at Hurst Park saw an unsatisfactory race for, although there were only six runners, both Atlas and China Rock seemed to be pocketed. Clichy, the runner-up, was at one time accidentally hit on the nose with a whip and, altogether, Atlas did well to come in third. Behind him was Zarathustra, and the winner was Hornbeam, both of whom were to feature in the dénouement of his career.

For the Queen held the hope that Atlas might crown her visit to Royal Ascot by winning the Gold Cup, and Carr, bearing Hurst Park in mind, turned down the prospect of riding Zarathustra to ride as usual for the Queen. Lester Piggott instead rode Zarathustra, having already ridden the winners of the 2,000 Guineas, the Derby, and the Oaks, a dazzling trio. Captain Boyd-Rochfort, too, was in an ironic position, for he had impartially trained two horses for the race, Atlas for the Queen and Zarathustra for Mr. Terence Gray.

The two and a half mile Gold Cup is not without resemblance to the King George VI and Queen Elizabeth Stakes in which High Veldt was still to have cause to hang his head in shame and, remarkably, Carr had Atlas in the lead for more than two miles of the way. Behind him was Hornbeam, French Beige, Tissot, Cambremer, and many others who had played their part in wrecking royal racing calculations in 1956. When Cambremer went rather wide, Piggott immediately took his chance and drove the jet-black Zarathustra between the French horse and Atlas. Seconds later, Piggott was a clear £1,000 better off by having won from Cambremer and Tissot with Hornbeam fourth and Atlas in fifth place. Sending for the winning owner, the Queen congratulated him with such sincerity and asked him so many questions about Zarathustra that he was charmed. Felicitously that summer afternoon the Queen already had a winner, for the incredible Pall Mall had earlier won the New Stakes worth £2,589. To end the story, Atlas was later sold to a syndicate to stand at the Hunsley House stud.

II

As on a chessboard the Queen and her racing management deployed their forces thoughtfully for the main attack of 1957. With the previous plan shattered, fresh strategies were launched, though the Queen could not have foreseen how strongly the tide of success was now flowing. Paying winter visits to Hurst Park, Newbury and Cheltenham with her mother, the Queen must have given a great deal of thought to her new racing stock. To lighten the load on Captain Moore's shoulders, Brigadier A. D. R. Wingfield was appointed the assistant manager of Her Majesty's stud at about this time and soon moved into Adelaide Cottage, the grace-and-favour house at Windsor where Peter Townsend once lived. Monkshood, Cheetah and Royal Taste were pruned from the former two-year-old string, leaving six horses in the new three-year-old group who were already for the most part of proved performance.

The colts Agreement, Doutelle and Lance-Corporal and the fillies Almeria, Mulberry Harbour and Sunburnt Country were the prospective classic winners the Queen now appraised at Freemason Lodge. Ten two-year-olds in addition and at least six promising yearlings were led out for her inspection one Saturday afternoon. Then there was her 4,000 guineas Doncaster purchase, the filly by Petition out of Danse d'Espoir, now neatly named Petronella. It may be added here that, despite many attempts, this sales buy did not win a race in two years.

At Warren Place six young tyros also faced their first racing season besides the doubtful Impala and the Dante–Calash filly, Carrozza, whom the Queen had personally selected at Gillingham, saying, 'I particularly like the look of her.' Visiting the Murless establishment, Her Majesty found much to praise, though unaware that her National Stud trainer would top the trainers' list that year with herself as champion-winning owner.

The golden trend began on the Queen's birthday eve when she motored from Windsor to Kempton Park with Princess Margaret and said mischievously to Captain Boyd-Rochfort, 'I would like a winner today, if you please, as a birthday present.'

Captain Boyd-Rochfort gave his usual courtly bow. With four runners Carr had at least high chances in his favour. Determined to have a good view of the triumph in store, Princess Margaret, to the Queen's amusement, climbed the high iron gangway of the judge's box and stood on the top step to watch the racing. With the second race, the Princess Royal Stakes, the Queen swung her binoculars back and forth from the runners to her venturesome sister. And the next moment Carr swept the two-year-old Migoli filly Might and Main past the post in an inextricable cluster of runners.

The Queen had to face the suspense of a photo finish before the judges decreed Might and Main second. 'We shall have to do better than that,' Her Majesty joked with her trainer. Though Doutelle was running in the big race of the day, the 2,000 Guineas Trial Stakes, her thoughts were probably pinned on Mulberry Harbour and Stenographer in the later races. Alexander and High Veldt had already won the 2,000 Guineas Trial in successive years and the Queen could hardly hope for a hat-trick.

Yet the miracle happened. The spirited little colt seemed to know exactly what was required of him and put on such a spurt against Super Snipe and Copenhagen that he won by one and a half lengths. Towards the end it could be seen that the Queen, completely absorbed, was riding him in imagination, her hands on the reins. The public cheered all the louder, with love and pleasure, seeing her dance with delight.

'The third time off the reel! It's almost unbelievable. Well done, Cecil!' she could be heard gaily exclaiming to the trainer.

It could have been enough for one day. It seemed sufficient in the next race when Stenographer, the two-year-old daughter of Fair Copy and Saucy Lass, merely came in third. But in the last race Carr had no difficulty in winning with Mulberry Harbour, half-sister to Alexander. She had been a little slow and made no score in the only two races she enjoyed as a two-year-old. Now she was quite effortlessly in the lead in the home run and drew away to win by four lengths.

'It's wonderful! A wonderful, wonderful day!' the Queen happily beamed at onlookers in the paddock, when she went there to renew her thanks to trainer and jockey. In the one day she had won stakes of nearly £2,000, so that Carr alone had cleared around £200. It could have been sufficient racing satisfaction for a week. The next day but one, however, the Queen again went to Kempton Park for the Easter Monday programme. Lunching with the stewards, Her Majesty was clearly not optimistic for her one runner, Agreement. Though a son of Persian Gulf–Northern Hope, he had been excessively backward in training. In his one and only race when at length given a try-out in October, he finished fifth of seven.

Offering £1,026 to the winner, the Coventry Three-Year-Old Stakes that afternoon was not without elements of opposition. Agreement none the less threw them off, took the lead in the straight and won from Mossarco by a length and a half. 'It's so unexpected!' cried the Queen, when the stewards congratulated her. 'He's only a baby!'

The tide had indeed turned with a swing. All the uncommended little-tried young hopefuls of 1956 suddenly began taking the 1957 honours as if a fairy godmother, aided and abetted by Captain Moore, had waved a magic wand.

Only a week or two divide the spring Kempton and Epsom meetings and the Queen returned from her Paris visit to further good news. Now Noel Murless was honoured to present Her Majesty with a winner. In the £6,471 Princess Elizabeth Stakes the Aga Khan's 1,000 Guineas favourite Rose Royale II was having a run and Alec Head, the trainer, did not anticipate very much trouble. Instead, Lester Piggott unmistakably won for the Queen on Carrozza.

The daughter of Dante–Calash started at 10–1 and it was her race all the way. Rose Royale II came on like a thunderbolt in the last hundred yards, but lost by half a length. At the same meeting, too, the Queen's Doncaster purchase, Stroma, made a good showing into second place in the Produce Stakes. And then came the right royal day at Haydock Park when the Queen for the first time, as I have already said, brought off a treble.

Haydock is not one of the largest venues and a royal horse may well have felt a stranger. A two-year-old beginner, Pall Mall, accordingly did not seem to know what it was all about when the tapes went up for the first race. Though he jumped off well, the scion of Palestine–Malapert ran green for a good two furlongs but then he drew away from the field. To the Queen, sailing aboard the *Britannia* on her State visit to Denmark with the Duke of Edinburgh, the news was swiftly flashed that Pall Mall had won by five lengths. Two hours later

Her Majesty received a message that Atlas had won the Haydock Park Stakes, breaking the course record for two miles with 3 minutes 30⅗ seconds. The Queen's elation could scarcely have died away than a third message was taken to the long desk in her private drawing-room. This time Might and Main had won the last race. Riding his third royal horse that afternoon Carr had got the filly away from the gate with such alacrity that all other challenges were readily held.

The Queen had now won nine races since the start of the season, an extremely satisfactory showing. Among other engagements, Agreement had come in second in the Rayner Stakes but had failed to concede five pounds to London Cry, the winner. Mulberry Harbour then won the Cheshire Oaks as favourite in a neck-and-neck finish from Crotchet. Tangibly in her grasp the Queen could see Mulberry Harbour in the Oaks and Doutelle in the Derby, these were in mind although the Queen had never yet had a classic winner.

Her Majesty went to Newmarket for the Guineas meeting, but the Royal Standard significantly did not fly above her box. Her visit, it was explained, was 'unofficial', and there could scarcely have been a stronger indication of the line which the Queen wished to be drawn between her round of duties and her private pursuits. Every morning the Queen rose so early at Sandringham that she was on Newmarket Heath for the gallops shortly after eight o'clock and, after watching the first work, she breakfasted at Freemason Lodge. Though Lance Corporal was to have aimed at the 2,000 Guineas, he was clearly in no sort of condition, and the Queen decided he should be scratched. It was thus left to 'the tax-payers' Carrozza' to represent the Queen in the 1,000 Guineas. On this occasion, however, Rose Royale II won equably and

Carrozza came in fourth just ahead of the Irish filly Silken Glider.

III

A new Epsom setting awaited the Queen as a backdrop to her hopes for Mulberry Harbour, Doutelle and — almost as a judicious afterthought — Carrozza. Gone was the draughty old Royal Box of the past. In its stead the Queen found a charming, modern set of apartments in silver-grey and dusky blue, a long dining-room and drawing-room, both close-carpeted and, the best of all innovations, a draught-averting glass lobby between the withdrawing-rooms and the glass balcony. Beaming with pleasure, the Queen made a tour of inspection of the prints of early Derby winners on the walls. The Derby winners of the twentieth century awaited her inspection in an album of photographs with blank pages for future years. Placing her finger on the first blank page, the Queen smilingly twice tapped but said not a word.

Doutelle to date had done precisely as required. At the Lingfield Derby Trial the threat was the Alycidon colt Alcastus, but Doutelle tracked him all the way, quickened at a touch from Carr in the last fifty yards and won by a neck. This said much for Mulberry Harbour, who had beaten Alcastus with still greater ease at Kempton Park. In the Oaks Trial, however, Almeria alone carried the royal silk, finishing third behind Crotchet and Lobelia.

Doutelle was easily the best-favoured royal Derby entrant for many years. Doubters studied the chestnut's parentage (Prince Chevalier–Above Board) and suggested that although the Prince Chevalier had marched on London he had got only as far as Derby. The crowds loudly cheered the procession of cars with the Queen, the Queen Mother, Princess Margaret, the

Princess Royal and the Duke and Duchess of Gloucester, and glibly explained the absence of the Duke of Edinburgh, 'He doesn't like racing, you know.' In point of fact, the Duke had flown to Germany to attend the wedding of his niece, Princess Margarita of Baden, an event arranged weeks before.

As we know, it was not Doutelle's Derby, but there will always remain a lingering, doubtful 'might have been'. Riding Doutelle, Carr found it the roughest Derby of his life. At four furlongs one horse, Bois de Miel, suddenly faltered. In seven starts Bois de Miel had not won a race, and it is difficult to see why he was kept in, except that it gave the American owner fun. When he dropped back half a dozen horses could not avoid an ensuing scramble. Rae Johnstone on Chippendale II could not get out of the way, Doutelle lost his stride and was bumped so roughly later on that it was found he sustained a damaged pastern. This kept him out of racing for some months. When the Queen congratulated Sir Victor Sassoon for winning with Crepello, she had quickly shrugged away Doutelle, finishing tenth, and was aware that Crepello had won only one and three-fifth second outside the course record. 'A splendid run!' she complimented Piggott, Crepello's jockey.

And the pundits had scarcely concluded the inquest on the Derby than they turned to the Oaks. Originally Almeria, Mulberry Harbour and Carrozza were entered, but the Queen decided to retain only the last two. Not for the first time Mulberry Harbour was hailed as the pick of the English fillies. Carrozza's chances were rated at 100–8. A royal horse had never won an Epsom Oaks. Indeed, a royal horse had not won an Epsom classic since Minoru's Derby. As trainer and rider of the Derby winner, Noel Murless and Piggott could scarcely anticipate that they would pocket the Oaks as well.

And what a wonderful race it was! At Tattenham Corner, Mulberry Harbour was second to Sir Victor Sassoon's Taittinger with Carrozza and Sarcelle just behind. Then Rose Royale II, the favourite, and Silken Glider, daughter of Airborne, swung up, while Taittinger still led, with Carrozza second. Three hundred yards from the post Piggott got to the front, but Silken Glider and Rose Royale II were closing up. At the firm ground the French favourite suddenly shirked, but it seemed certain that Silken Glider would gain on Carrozza. Two strides *beyond* the post Piggott knew that Silken Glider was a neck in front and thought he had lost. The loudspeaker announcement of 'Photograph for first place' led to a hush that could be felt.

The mighty roar that went up with the decision that Carrozza had won set the horse jibbing. The photograph showed a clear win of nine inches. But when the Queen took her filly's leading-rein Carrozza dug in her toes and moved backward and for a moment people feared for the Queen's safety.

To be sure, Noel Murless was close at hand and Piggott up. But the Queen immediately saw that the horse was alarmed by the battery of Press cameras. Wheeling Carrozza to one side with practised hand she obscured the filly's view and Carrozza followed meekly. Characteristically the Queen immediately enquired about Mulberry Harbour, who had finished ninth. At Tattenham Corner, the Boyd-Rochfort filly had in fact dropped out with an abruptness that recalled the Devon Loch incident. So sudden was her collapse that Carr feared she was lame, but she picked up and went on, though in distress. Subsequently, slight signs of heart strain were detected, but it proved to be nothing that rest could not put right.

Like battle casualties, indeed, several of the Queen's horses were soon on the Freemason Lodge easy list. Doutelle and

Mulberry Harbour were quickly joined by Agreement, who displayed highly disagreeable traits at exercise one morning when he attempted to make a meal of his lead-horse Michelino. Turning on the unoffending leader he tore a great hole in his exercise sheet with his teeth and the two were well into a scrap before Bruce Hobbs could reach them.

Michelino kicked back and the pair bucked and fought their way across the road and into a plantation. Michelino perhaps seemed to win on points, for Agreement fell through the ropes in the shape of a handy fence. Afterwards Agreement was gelded and it was a much meeker animal who returned to racing later in the year to take a third place at Brighton. His changed status was eventually to have a strange sequel. But Agreement made a decisive comeback when he won the Newmarket St. Leger prize of £1,382 and then topped this by a two-length win of the Lowther Stakes. In the latter only three ran. The runner-up was the Alycidon colt Cannebiere. The third and last home, the Queen may have noted with interest, was another Persian Gulf gelding, Red Influence.

Doutelle, similarly, did not reappear until the Cumberland Lodge at Ascot in October, when once again it was merely a three-cornered struggle. The five-year-old Poaching dropped back after an early lead, leaving Doutelle to win by a length and a half from Bellborough. Once again the Queen was winning owner after a see-saw struggle with Sir Victor Sassoon through the year. Once again Doutelle had proved a successor to Aureole (who won the Cumberland in 1953) and the news was radioed to the Queen *en route* in her airliner to Canada. It was a favourable omen.

In the Limekiln Stakes, equally, Doutelle made all the running to win from Rose Argent and Tempest, leaving his stable companion, Mulberry Harbour, far behind. The doughty colt was then invited to Laurel Park where his triumph might have supplied a glittering footnote to the resounding success of the Queen's own American visit. But when Mr. McKeldin, the Governor of Maryland, personally gave the invitation to the Queen, Her Majesty smilingly declined. Ballymoss, runner-up in the Derby and 1957 winner of the St Leger (which the Queen did not attend), was also entered as a British runner, and 'it would not be sporting', the Queen explained, to have one of her horses in it too.

To return to the hospital squad, however, it was finally joined, albeit briefly, by Carrozza when she had the misfortune to spread a plate while under starter's orders for the Nassau Stakes at Goodwood. The starter elected that the horse should go on ... and on three shoes, tender where a nail had penetrated her foot, Carrozza still ran gamely on and finished fourth. She was, however, lame, and the Queen looked much concerned.

Her Majesty finished the year with the total of £62,212 gained as winning owner from the stakes of sixteen wins in thirty races. The remarkable fact remains that Carrozza contributed no less than £22,562 of this sum, despite the many fine victories of the Queen's home-bred horses.

16: AGREEMENT AND ALMERIA

I

Only one owner had two winners at the 1957 Royal Ascot and only one owner had the good fortune of four winners during Ascot Week, if one may include the informal Heath meeting on the Saturday. In each case it was the Queen's 'purple, gold braid, scarlet sleeves' that slipped repeatedly first past the post, the symptom of an Ascot of peerless June sunshine freed at last from oppressive international rivalry. Only four of the week's prizes went overseas. After less than a decade of ownership, Her Majesty could see her untiring zeal for the supremacy of the British thoroughbred showing the dividends of prestige, always the true gauge of her pleasure and satisfaction. Many great Irish and French challenges were still to be met, many fresh dangers still to be faced and overcome. Yet it now became clear that royal bloodstock would wield a profound influence on British racing for many years to come.

Through Ascot Week, it is said, the Queen kept a little china horse near her for luck. Prince Charles had bought it for her out of his pocket-money, and when the Queen left it behind in the car an equerry was sent to fetch it post-haste. Talisman or not, the Hampton filly Almeria won the Ribblesdale Stakes by five lengths, and the Queen, richly pleased, hurried to the unsaddling enclosure with such eagerness that she arrived before the horse. Personal friendships enhanced the afternoon, for Lady Zia Wernher's Retrial won the Royal Hunt Cup, as the royal Alexander had done the previous year, and the top of the paddock assumed the usual atmosphere of a gay family party. The following afternoon, when Atlas lost the Gold Cup,

215

the two-year-old Pall Mall supplied compensation by winning the New Stakes in a hard-fought finish. Then, at the end of the week, the five-year-old Michelino, running as an outsider, won the Halifax Stakes and the National Stud youngster, Flake White, consolidated the Queen's position in the Fenwolf Stakes.

But perhaps Almeria was the true china horse, the surprise out of the bag. Her only other races, her third place as a two-year-old in the Waterford Stakes and her green run to finish third behind Crotchet and Lobelia in the Oaks Trial, hardly seemed to some to justify her advance to clear favourite for the Ribblesdale. On her next appearance, in the Bentinck Stakes at Goodwood, Carr had never seemed more confident of a win in his life. Motoring down from London that morning, the Queen and the Duke of Edinburgh were held up in the traffic like ordinary mortals but arrived in time to share his enthusiasm.

The second favourite, Hindu Festival, had the merit of having run second to Ballymoss in the Irish Derby. The Bentinck is run over one and three-quarter miles, and for half that distance Almeria plodded quietly second to this rival. Then she picked up when Carr asked and won by most of a length with Double Red third.

Close behind Carrozza's £22,562 that year, in fact, Almeria won £17,792 for the Queen in four races. The Queen was at Balmoral when the news came that her Alycidon–Avila filly had taken the best prize yet, the £6,938 total of the Yorkshire Oaks, practically walking away from her old rivals, Blue Galleon and Crotchet, with a win of six lengths. This was followed with the Park Hill Stakes at Doncaster, two days after Ballymoss's St. Leger, this time defeating Crotchet and Silken Glider.

Thus garlanded with laurels, it was decided to retire her to stud at Hampton. Shrewd judges had pronounced her the best-staying filly in Europe and she might indeed have won Carrozza's Oaks, offering the fates an interesting alternative. The Newmarket Oaks still remained, but Almeria was found to have pulled a muscle and the stud decision stood. Yet she was destined to make an astonishing comeback.

That was the autumn of Her Majesty's first visit to Canada as Queen; and in the United States her American hosts thoughtfully arranged a day of racing interest when she drove to the Middleburgh training track. Eighteen of the finest yearlings of Virginia were led out for her inspection, together with the retired chase champion, Elkridge, while as a leading horsewoman Mrs. M. E. Lunn had the invidious task of commentating the parade. The Queen watched appreciatively. But one imagines that no parade could have vied with the stocktaking of winners whose triumphs were already safely booked in the racing ledgers at home.

Besides those enumerated, it was the two-year-old royal filly Candytuft that picked up the £470 Alfriston Stakes at Brighton first time out and thus enabled Noel Murless to top his stakes winnings to above the record of £93,899 built up by Joe Lawson in 1931. Nor was this a fluke, for Candytuft shortly afterwards won again at Birmingham. Petronella, one of the Queen's Doncaster purchases, on the other hand was merely runner-up twice and gained a third place once in her three races. Lance Corporal failed the obligations of his royal silk when Her Majesty visited the Newmarket July meeting for the first time, but he did better later. Among others, Almeria's younger sister, Alesia, and even the six-year-old Opera Score all provided a due quota of victories. Altogether the Queen won twenty-three races with eleven horses, representing a percentage among British owners that only Lord Rosebery narrowly exceeded.

II

Returning to England, the Queen lost little time in visiting Hampton to inspect Almeria, and found the intended mare placidly munching in the paddocks showing no sign of her former muscle strain. The veterinary surgeons agreed that she was indeed in perfect health again and could race another season. So instead of enjoying the pleasures of motherhood Almeria found herself back at Newmarket in Boyd-Rochfort's major training string, a change that did not appeal to her at all.

She became difficult at about this time, mulishly digging her toes in whenever she saw signs of being led to the gallops. The skilled blandishments of her stable-girl, Valerie Frost, often proved of no avail and Danny Barnett, the head lad, frequently had to take over. Once she started, Carr found, she needed little urging, especially on the Long Hill run. It was simply that Almeria was sick of the sight of the limekilns and the racecourse gallops. She had to be coaxed and cajoled and Captain Boyd-Rochfort had an anxious time, wondering whether her tantrums could be controlled on the racecourse.

It was May before a suitable event could be found for her first appearance of the year, but then her comeback in the Coombe Stakes at Sandown Park was most impressive. The weights seemed to favour her old Goodwood rival, Double Red, and the race of nearly one and three-quarter miles was a keen test of staying power. Both Almeria and Double Red drew away from the rest and Lindley on Double Red was content to shadow the Queen's horse until the last furlong. Then he accelerated, but Almeria also put on a spurt and it was always clearly her win.

That Whitsun weekend, too, there were misleading signs and portents, for Almeria's stable companion, Agreement, was away at Redcar in a race which he inconspicuously lost. At Freemason Lodge, however, the filly and the gelding were now not infrequently teamed together at exercise. When Agreement acted as pacemaker, it was found, the filly enjoyed his company and usually behaved. After all, perhaps all she needed was a friend.

Agreement, too, freshly interested his owner, for he seemed well able to stay with Almeria over a distance, and the Queen earlier decided to try him in the mile-and-a-quarter Great 'Jubilee' Handicap at Kempton Park. That weekend the Queen and Prince Philip were staying with their close friends, Lieut.-Colonel and Mrs. Harold Phillips, in Leicestershire. When it drizzled with rain the Queen suggested that it might be fun to watch the Jubilee on television. Unluckily, with four children to control, the Phillips had decided against having television in the house.

John Kemp, the butler, however, had a set in his nearby cottage and declared that he would indeed be honoured if the Queen cared to watch. Perhaps it is the only occasion on or off the record when a Queen has sat cosily in an armchair in a butler's sitting-room watching television, but the Queen saw Agreement finish eighth, discussed the race with keen enjoyment and did not forget to thank her butler-host.

Then at Royal Ascot, Agreement was tried over the mile and a half of the Bessborough Stakes, but he could not stay against the Hyperion gelding Huguenot and came in second. What was worse, perhaps, was that Almeria abandoned the manners she had learned with Agreement and refused to gallop either with or without him.

Though not running at Royal Ascot she had been brought to the course at the Queen's special request for a good trial over the King George VI and Queen Elizabeth course. Her Majesty brought a dozen members of her Windsor house-party to watch, and could not but make wry jokes when Almeria stubbornly refused to jump off with the other horses.

After two false starts, Carr finally got her going, but still she merely ambled lengths behind the others, refusing to be persuaded.

Could she possibly be trusted against Ballymoss in the great Ascot £28,000 mile and a half? Was she worth running as a second to Doutelle or perhaps the three-year-old Miner's Lamp? Both colts were entered, but the final acceptance, as racegoers remember, saw Almeria and Doutelle pitted against Al Mabsoot, Brioche, China Rock, Thila, Hard Ridden and Ballymoss.

Once again the Queen watched by television, staying at home under doctor's orders. Perhaps Her Majesty thus failed to notice that the stable-girl who led Almeria around the paddock loyally wore a hairband in the royal racing colours of red, purple and gold. But the cameras clearly showed Almeria backing away from the starting-gate, obdurate until Carr dismounted and led her up.

Then the tapes went up and Almeria flashed in front. It may long be argued that if Doutelle had been harder ridden to help force the pace the Queen's filly might have won. She led into the straight with Doutelle, Ballymoss and Hard Ridden, the Derby winner, behind her. It was only when she eased imperceptibly for a vital second that Ballymoss darted forward and his long raking stride carried him into his win, three lengths ahead of Almeria with Doutelle third.

'That's what I would call a horse and a half, a very fine horse indeed!' the Queen Mother warmly congratulated the owner, John McShain. Yet Doutelle, too, it was noted, had not unvaliantly outrun the current Derby winner as well as Al Mabsoot, the runner-up in the 'King and Queen' the previous year.

III

The Queen always learns from racing defeats, and there were still laurels for Almeria to salvage during the season. A pacemaker, however, was a paramount need and the choice remained crucial. Convalescing from her sinus trouble, the Queen missed the first two days of Goodwood, but on the third day she received a tremendous ovation. Both Doutelle and Almeria were entered for the Goodwood Cup, but the filly did not appear. In her absence, Doutelle was rated second favourite, chiefly on his appearance in the Ormonde at Chester when he beat Ballymoss into second place.

The Goodwood Cup has not been won by the reigning monarch since William IV and, as it turned out, the scoffers jeered that Doutelle might equally have stayed at home, for he came in last. In reality, he had been struck into and finished lame. Stroma, too, was drubbed in the Singleton Handicap that day into the last of twelve. Though Goodwood was peppered with royal runners, from Pall Mall to Persian Wheel, Sundown and Short Sentence, not one achieved a win.

In the end nothing remained but to set Agreement as pacemaker to Almeria in the Doncaster Cup. Four failures in the year had reduced the gelding's status to that of a 25–1 outsider. The stable knew that the Queen was particularly anxious to see Almeria win and thus cap the victory of Atlas in

1956. But as the day of the race drew near anxiety ensued, for Almeria went slightly amiss.

With three days to go, with two days to go, she was still not in perfect form. She was nevertheless prepared for the journey to Doncaster just in case and stepped demurely into her travelling van while an overnight tipster noted, 'The Queen's Almeria can beat Hornbeam in today's Doncaster Cup *if* she runs … particularly as the Queen's Agreement will no doubt ensure the good pace which is so necessary.' It was a mightily relieved trainer who discovered at last that Almeria would be able to run.

Many lucky folk were on to Almeria with a few pounds on Agreement as a 'saver'. With a field of seven, she started as the 5–2 joint favourite with Hornbeam, who had fought out the finish with French Beige the previous year. On the way to the post Almeria was a little fractious, but all went well. Passing the stands it was seen that Agreement and Almeria were lying first and second with Agreement setting a steady gallop as had been intended.

The French Ranchiquito drew back and French Beige pulled forward. Almeria and Agreement were nearly in line — but then a devastating and drastically unexpected thing happened.

Almeria coyly refused to pass her endearing stable friend. She kept level with him, but nothing Carr could do would urge her forward to pass him. Yard by yard she kept level, far ahead of the rest of the field, and then the crowd prepared to cheer the victory of a royal favourite abruptly fell into stunned silence as Agreement drew away to win by a neck. The pacemaker had indeed set the pace only too well. Doug Smith on Agreement won the Doncaster Cup for the sixth time since the war, but it was his least expected win of all. As for Almeria, she was indeed firmly retired to stud at Hampton, never more to return.

More happily, Agreement also went on to win the Chester Cup in 1959 and so the large 'first place' cheese that Atlas had missed duly graced the Queen's table after all, minus a sizeable chunk that was thoughtfully sent to Captain Boyd-Rochfort.

17: PALL MALL TO AUGUSTINE

I

In 1958 the Queen won twenty-one races with six horses and her stakes winnings totalled £47,415, a figure that would have topped the list but for the Ascot loss to Ballymoss. As a breeder, too, Her Majesty had the pleasure of noting that her Hampton horses built up wins of £39,625, the third figure on the breeders' list of the year. In that year also Harry Carr suitably notched his thousandth win under Jockey Club rules by riding Alesia, Almeria's sister, home to a six-length victory at Brighton. The fact remains that until 1958 the Queen had never won a classic with a horse of her very own.

Quite suddenly the Queen decided that she had a possible winner of the 2,000 Guineas in Pall Mall. As a two-year-old Pall Mall always ran reliably and won his first two races only to fall just short of top honours in the next three. After winning the New Stakes at Royal Ascot, for instance, he was second in the Newmarket July Stakes, third in the Gimcrack and then was second to Kelly by a short head after a wonderful race in the Champagne Stakes at Doncaster.

On the chilly Easter Saturday when Windsor Park was waterlogged and Kempton Park racecourse still soft from recent slush, the Queen, the Queen Mother and Princess Margaret went to see the colt in the 2,000 Guineas Trial Stakes. It was a race that Captain Boyd-Rochfort had won five times in succession — and three times with the Queen's horses — though he had never won the 2,000 Guineas itself. But every run of luck eventually expires, and the Queen and her trainer had the bleak experience of watching Pall Mall run to fourth place, eight lengths behind the winner, Sir Harold Wernher's Aggressor.

Oddly enough, Aggressor had also endured the affront of being offered for sale and failing to sell. Sent to auction as a yearling, the top bid of 750 guineas was below Sir Harold's reserve and he was withdrawn. Yet Captain Boyd-Rochfort, with first choice of the Wernher horses, also ignored him and he was trained by J. M. Gosden at Lewes. None of the first three had been entered for the classics. The runner-up, Sir Winston Churchill's Welsh Abbot, was rated at 6–1. Though trained at Freemason Lodge, Sir Humphrey de Trafford's Mr. Snake, third, had not appeared for a year. Nevertheless Carr found excuses for the light-actioned Pall Mall, who was always a different horse on top of the ground.

'He found it far too soft for him, ma'am,' the jockey told the Queen.

So Pall Mall was given another chance in the Thirsk Classic Trial just before the Queen's birthday with Rickaby up. Battling with Pleiades, the son of Nearco, he won by a length. And, incidentally, Doutelle also cleaned up the John Porter Stakes at Newbury that day, the first royal victories of the season, giving Her Majesty the welcome birthday gift of a double.

Could Pall Mall also bring in the 2,000 Guineas? The pundits recalled that Nearula and Nimbus had won at Thirsk before going on to take the Newmarket classic. They remembered, too, that Captain Boyd-Rochfort had never yet trained a 2,000 Guineas winner. Eager to go to Newmarket, the Queen had to stay at Windsor owing to a heavy cold, and her aunt, the Princess Royal, was the only member of the Royal Family to watch Pall Mall's triumphant run.

At 20–1 he was cynically rated an outsider, and at his gallops he had always seemed markedly inferior to his stable companion, the American-owned Bald Eagle, who was dominant favourite. Riding a waiting race to give his colt every chance for the mile, Doug Smith must have been fortified by memories of his former royal win on Hypericum, that runaway race that had so thrilled the young Princess Elizabeth. Down the hill Pall Mall quickened at each little whisk of the whip, neck and neck with Eph Smith on Major Portion on the far side. And ultimately Pall Mall won by half a length while the famous Bald Eagle was lying seventh.

At Windsor the Queen was jubilant. Noel Murless was reminded that a Guineas double might be possible by winning the 1,000 Guineas with the royal National Stud mare Persian Wheel. This daughter of Tulyar and Sun Chariot did no better than fourth, however, in a strung-out field. But now that first Meld in the 1,000 and Pall Mall in the 2,000 had thoroughly broken the Guineas hoodoo for Boyd-Rochfort, why not a Derby winner at long last for Freemason Lodge? And why not a portrait of Her Majesty's Derby winner to hang above the green armchairs in the Captain's study?

II

The week before the 2,000 Guineas, another royal newcomer was tried out in the Blue Riband Trial, that alleged Epsom precursor of the Derby. Miner's Lamp, a colt by Signal Light out of the Hampton dam Young Entry and thus a half-brother to Atlas, regularly and forcefully tried to climb his stable door as an angry young man's symptom of resentment, but could he walk away with the Derby after he had demolished the stable door?

The Blue Riband featured as a race which Captain Boyd-Rochfort had already won four times in five years, and Atlas was his one failure. Miner's Lamp had the same chestnut sheen but he came in a larger size with an unelegant long back, and he entered the Derby as a dark horse at 25–1. He had previously appeared in only one race as a two-year-old, becoming a runner-up three lengths behind Sir Victor Sassoon's Pinched in the Royal Lodge Stakes. But in his private life at Freemason Lodge, though quiet as a sheep, he was a climber, standing on his hind legs to tear down the electric lamps, rending his rugs to shreds.

He was a clear case, in fact, for the tranquillizing influence of Charles Brook, the 'tamer of Aureole'. When treatment started in early February, the stable felt that Miner's Lamp seemed unlikely to be risked on the course again. Four times a week the persistent, grey-bearded Mr. Brook visited this new patient, sometimes admittedly not too happy at being closeted with such a firework. Then Miner's Lamp won the Blue Riband Trial in unmistakable style by an easy four lengths and his Derby price promptly shortened to 10–1.

Next came the Newmarket Stakes, when Miner's Lamp was currently third Derby favourite, a race that saw him squarely defeated by Guersillus and reduced to second place by three lengths. His Derby price promptly went to 20–1, but the trainers knew that the Queen was no less interested in the Lingfield Derby Trial, in which the Murless-trained Snow Cat — half-brother to Carrozza — was running against Sir Humphrey de Trafford's Alcide. When the latter won by twelve long lengths, leaving Snow Cat at fourth place, the Queen eliminated Snow Cat from her Epsom hopes. This left Miner's Lamp, while Noel Murless still represented the Queen with Persian Wheel in the Oaks.

When Her Majesty went to Newmarket Heath to watch the work in the pre-Derby week — and incidentally to record much of the exercise with her movie camera — the issue remained cloudier than ever, for the favourite Alcide had pulled a stomach muscle. Yet everyone knows how the Derby field was whittled down until eventually the great classic was won by Sir Victor Sassoon's Hard Ridden, a horse bought in Dublin for only 270 guineas as a yearling.

'He is so quiet you could ride him for Trooping the Colour,' Sir Victor told the Queen.

'I should be terrified,' laughed Her Majesty.

Many spectators in the Royal Box were clearly dismayed at seeing Miner's Lamp come in sixth with the bunch, but the Queen so seldom reveals disappointment. Miner's Lamp made amends when he effortlessly won the Princess of Wales's Stakes at Newmarket. Snow Cat atoned for her own earlier defeat when she won the Rous Memorial Stakes at Royal Ascot, Eph Smith's first royal win since he won the George VI and Queen Elizabeth with Aureole. The Queen was so pleased that she attempted to shake his hand before he weighed-in. Hurriedly the jockey backed away, touching his cap.

Though Persian Wheel lost the Oaks, a dismal eighth, she still picked up the gentler Falmer Stakes. Though Restoration proved a not unworthy fourth in the St. Leger, he had already fully shown himself a dutiful son of Persian Gulf-Hypericum, with his superb and unforgettable photo finish against Arctic Explorer as runner-up in the Eclipse Stakes.

And then there was Doutelle's half-brother, Above Suspicion; the valiant Sundown, full brother to High Veldt; the filly Blue Riband; Ibrox, half-sister to Agreement ... and so to Kerry Hill, the daughter of Astrakhan. And still they come, a lasting pageant on the green cloth of the Turf, the powerful

Optimistic, the striding Square Acre, the patch-faced lovable Augustine, son of Aureole. There will be the foals of Almeria and Mulberry Harbour, of Alesia and Petronella. Now, at the revived royal stud at Sandringham, Aureole and Doutelle stand, stabled with right royal sentiment close to the statue of Persimmon.

Here's a health unto Her Majesty, as she each year opens a new chapter of racing drama and each year looks happily back through a racing ledger filled with fresh achievement. For the Queen, as for all of us, royal racing brings the lasting fascination of past records and the perennial anticipations of the future.

ACKNOWLEDGEMENTS

The author wishes to express special thanks to H.M. Queen Elizabeth the Queen Mother for her gracious permission to quote from Her Majesty's personal racing records. The author's grateful acknowledgement of kindness and help is also due to Captain Charles Moore, C.V.O., M.C., Racing Manager to H.M. The Queen; Captain C. C. Boyd-Rochfort, C.V.O., Mr. Peter Cazalet, and the establishment of Mr. Noel Murless, trainers for H.M. the Queen or H.M. Queen Elizabeth the Queen Mother; as well as to other individuals of Her Majesty's racing personnel and the various members of the Royal Households who so courteously assisted in the preparation of this book.

A NOTE TO THE READER

If you have enjoyed this book enough to leave a review on **Amazon** and **Goodreads**, then we would be truly grateful.
The Estate of Helen Cathcart

Sapere Books is an exciting new publisher of brilliant fiction and popular history.

To find out more about our latest releases and our monthly bargain books visit our website: **saperebooks.com**